Cambridg

CW01432580

Text Analysis and Representation

Ian Cushing

Series Editors: Dan Clayton and Marcello Giovanelli

CAMBRIDGE
UNIVERSITY PRESS

University Printing House, Cambridge CB2 8BS, United Kingdom

One Liberty Plaza, 20th Floor, New York, NY 10006, USA

477 Williamstown Road, Port Melbourne, VIC 3207, Australia

314–321, 3rd Floor, Plot 3, Splendor Forum, Jasola District Centre, New Delhi – 110025, India

79 Anson Road, #06–04/06, Singapore 079906

Cambridge University Press is part of the University of Cambridge.

It furthers the University's mission by disseminating knowledge in the pursuit of education, learning and research at the highest international levels of excellence.

www.cambridge.org
Information on this title: www.cambridge.org/9781108401111

© Cambridge University Press 2018

First published 2018

20 19 18 17 16 15 14 13 12 11 10 9 8 7 6 5 4 3 2 1

Printed in Malaysia by Vivar Printing

A catalogue record for this publication is available from the British Library

ISBN 978-1-108-40111-1 Paperback

Cambridge University Press has no responsibility for the persistence or accuracy of URLs for external or third-party internet websites referred to in this publication, and does not guarantee that any content on such websites is, or will remain, accurate or appropriate.

....

Contents

Series introduction

Cambridge Topics in English Language is a series of accessible introductory study guides to major scholarly topics in the fields of English language and linguistics. These books have been designed for use by students at advanced level and beyond and provide detailed overviews of each topic together with the latest research in the field so as to provide a clear introduction that is both practical and up to date.

In all of the books in this series, we have drawn on examples of spoken and written language. We hope these will encourage you to apply the theories, concepts and methods that you will learn in the books to analyse data and to think critically about a number of issues and debates relating to language in use. Many of the books also draw on data from the Cambridge Corpus. Throughout each book, you will find short activities to help develop reading and writing skills, longer extended activities and practice questions that will enable you to explore your learning in more detail and research findings that will provide inspiration for your own language investigations. Each of the chapters includes suggested wider reading, and a full glossary and reference section at the end of each book will support you to extend your learning and provide avenues for future reading and research.

We hope that each book will give you a good overview of its topic and, that taken as a whole, the series will map out some of the most interesting and diverse areas of language study, providing you with fresh thinking and new ideas as you embark on your studies.

Dan Clayton

Marcello Giovanelli

How to use this book

Throughout this book you will notice recurring features that are designed to help your learning. Here is a brief overview of what you'll find.

> **Coverage list**
>
> A short list of what you will learn in each chapter.

> **KEY TERM**
>
> Definitions of important terms to help your understanding of the topic.

> **ACTIVITY**
>
> A clearly defined task to help you apply what you've learnt.

> **RESEARCH QUESTION**
>
> A longer task to help you go deeper into the topic.

> **PRACTICE QUESTION**
>
> To give you some practice of questions you might encounter in the exam.

Ideas and answers

Further information, suggestions and answers to all activities and practice questions in the book.

Wider reading

Key texts to help extend your learning.

Topic introduction

In writing this book, I have tried to do a number of things. The main objective (as you might have guessed from the title) is to provide suggestions and methods for analysing texts. In doing so, I will outline some principles and approaches concerning language study, and apply these to real-life language in authentic contexts. I also hope that this book serves as a general introduction to English linguistics – the study of present-day English from a number of different angles. Finally, I hope that this book provides you with a way of *thinking* about language.

There is no 'one way' to read this book – but I do encourage you to read it as a mixture of theory and practice. The analyses of texts* that I offer are my own, and I offer these not as absolute answers, but as mere suggestions and interpretations. I encourage you to be critical of these, and to develop interpretations of your own: text analysis is an activity, and the best way to learn is by doing.

It is *not* a book on formal linguistics (a branch of linguistics concerned with abstract properties of language, and has little to offer in analysing the way that speech and writing creates meaning), but it does offer some tools that will help you to describe the structure and systems of English. It is not a rulebook or a grammar book: there are plenty of those that already exist.

There are lots of different approaches to analysing texts, and lots of different approaches to doing linguistics. In a book of this length, I cannot possibly cover all of these – and for those that I can cover, I can only provide general introductions. The suggestions for further reading should satisfy your curiosities to explore things in more depth.

Finally, I encourage you to have fun with language: use this book as a springboard to explore its flexibility, its power and its oddities, and above all, its enduring characteristic of how meanings are made.

*There is a transcription key at the end of the book to help you with the texts.

Ian Cushing

Topic introduction

Chapter 1
What is text analysis and representation?

In this chapter you will:

- Establish an understanding of discourse, context, text and representation

- Explore some approaches to studying language

- Consider the importance of context

- Develop an understanding of what text analysis looks like

Text Analysis and Representation

1.1 Big issues

The aim of this book is to equip you with the linguistic skills required to analyse written and spoken language. We will be concerned with how language works to create meanings, and in doing so, we will consider some 'big', fundamental issues in language study, which will be our starting point. We start here because these big issues in language cannot – and should not – be ignored when it comes to conducting good text analysis. Big issues then, are those that are relevant to every instance of language use, and are actually a very good way to consider how meanings are made in any text. The big issues are the starting point of this book for a reason – they are the starting point when it comes to analysing language.

Perhaps the best way to exemplify these 'big issues' then, is to start with a text. Read Text 1A through a couple of times, and think about what you notice in terms of language. Also think about *where* you would see such a text (which is starting to think about context).

> **KEY TERM**
>
> **Context:** the background against which a text conveys its meaning

Text 1A

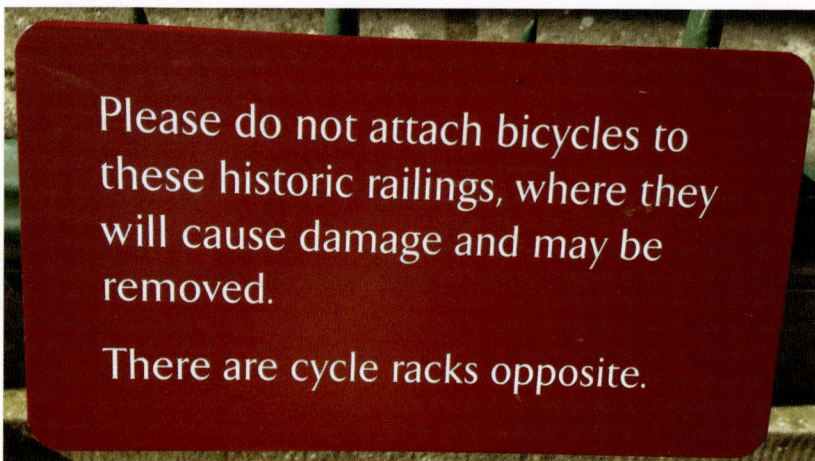

Please do not attach bicycles to these historic railings, where they will cause damage and may be removed.

There are cycle racks opposite.

This, admittedly, is a seemingly straightforward text. On first impressions, it's certainly not the most exciting thing to read in the world, and when I stopped to take a photograph of it, I'm sure people watching me wondered why I wasn't taking a photograph of the historic building behind the railings (which is what everyone else was doing). The reason that I did take a photograph of it though, is because I consider myself a keen observer of language – and I would like to encourage you to be the same. Despite its simplicity, there are some interesting things to say here, in terms of the big language issues.

1.2 Discourse

When you read the text, I asked you to consider where you thought it might 'come from'. Although you might not have guessed the complete details, you probably had a rough idea. Or certainly a good idea of where you *wouldn't* see such a text. The photo was taken outside a Cambridge University building, and the sign was attached to some (historic) railings. As you might have guessed, the building that the railings were protecting was also historic, and required payment to enter. The sign is protecting two things: the physical, historic railings from any potential damage, but also the more abstract idea of privacy and exclusivity of space. Because the building is owned by the university, an institution with political and financial 'weight', they have the power and authority to produce such texts. In turn, these texts control and regulate the way people behave. In this way, the text is 'performing' an action: it's imposing a limit on what you can and cannot do.

Cambridge is a prestigious and well-thought-of university, famous throughout the world. Tourists come to the city to see the kinds of historic buildings (and railings) that Text 1A is designed to protect. Many buildings are thought of as architecturally impressive, and visitors would generally behave in a way that respects this: not graffitiing on the walls, not throwing stones at the windows, and so on. The fact that the railings themselves are protected gives you a clue to just how seriously the university looks after its own property! However, Cambridge is also a city popular with cyclists, so the text also presumes that the railings are likely to be targeted by people looking for a good place to lock up their bike. Similar kinds of signs around the university building also help to understand how the text is working: Text 1A is part of a much wider discourse of Cambridge itself, a city that prides itself on its presentation, heritage and unspoilt architecture, and one that is popular with cyclists. As you walk around the city and encounter lots of these kinds of signs, your own knowledge and understanding of that discourse is further established and built on.

KEY TERM

Discourse: the analysis of a) how language in use creates meanings; b) natural language occurring in different social contexts; c) how language is used as a form of social practice

1

Discourse can be a tricky concept to define, and many different understandings and definitions exist. Most definitions would include the following three elements, and these are the ones we will assume for the rest of this book:

1   Discourse is about how language creates meaning.

2   Discourse is language in use.

3   Discourse is a form of social practice, in which language plays a central role.

Discourse can be a messy and complex aspect of text analysis – but it is also fascinating and fundamental to understanding how texts work. Engaging with discourse allows us to see how language actually operates in society, to understand how societal structures and practices affect language usage, or discourse events. James Paul Gee (2014) suggests that doing discourse analysis is 'walking the walk *and* talking the talk'. By this, he means that language is just one part of text analysis: readers, writers, speakers, hearers, society and ideology are all important parts too. In doing discourse analysis then, you will be analysing how language, actions, interactions, power, ways of thinking, believing, valuing and using various symbols, tools and objects create a particular sort of socially recognisable identity.

KEY TERM

Discourse event: an act of communication occurring in a specific time and location involving writers/speakers and readers/listeners

1.3 Context

If discourse is a big part of language analysis, then it may be useful to think of context as a kind of smaller category within it. The word 'context' is formed from the Latin *con-*, meaning 'together'. So context points to the things that come *with* the text; the situation through which language use occurs and is understood. It is defined by 'local' contextual parameters: the *when*, *where*, *who* and *why* of a text. As a part of discourse, context further shapes the way that language is used and determines how meanings are made. So, the contextual parameters that make up this text include:

- **Time**: produced at some point after the railings were built, perhaps after bicycles were found attached.

- **Place**: outside a building owned by Cambridge University.

- **Audience**: potentially anybody that passes, but specifically people who are thinking of attaching their bicycle there.

- **Writer**: unknown, but presumably somebody working for the university's heritage and sites office.

- **Purpose or function**: to dictate the 'local laws' and limitations as set out by the university.

> **KEY TERM**
>
> **Contextual parameters:** specific time, location, person and function details about the context of a text: *when, where, who* and *why*

Contextual parameters are then, more specific than things at the discourse level. They all, in turn, shape the language of a text, which shapes meaning. It might appear that discourse and context can be 'everything', which not only makes text analysis seem very daunting, but also impossible. So, try to exercise some control when analysing texts: whilst they are fundamental parts of the analytical process, remember that you can only do so much. A good place to start is to ask basic questions such as:

- Who produced the text, and why?

- What is the text telling me or suggesting I do?

- Where might you read or hear such a text?

The important thing to remember is that discourse and context have enormous influence on the ways that language is used, representations are created, and meanings are made.

1.4 Meaning

Now that we've explored the notion of discourse and looked at the context of Text 1A, we turn our attention to the construction of meaning – how a text means what it does. We will do this by looking at the language of the text in light of its context and the way it is understood by language users. Some technical linguistic terminology will be introduced here, but Chapters 2 and 3 of this book will discuss the structure of language in more detail. Generally then, Text 1A means something along the lines of 'these railings are historic; bicycles can cause damage to them; do not attach your bicycle here'. But it only means this, in the context that we discussed earlier.

In exploring meaning, a good place to start is thinking about who created the text, otherwise known as the text producer. Looking again at Text 1A, there's certainly no individual name attributed to the text, but the fact that the sign is stuck outside a building owned by Cambridge University means that there is

Text Analysis and Representation

instead an institutional author. This is done for a reason: it isn't a personal text and there's no attempt to create a relationship with its audience, apart from the attempt to appear polite by starting the text with 'please'. In fact, the institution wants to remain quite 'distant' from their audience, in order to appear powerful and authoritative. It would be strange if the text ended with something like 'Cheers, Jim', and a sign-off like this would probably change the meaning, in that the text wouldn't appear quite so serious and be less efficient in its intended purpose of detracting people wishing to lock their bike up. All texts have a text producer, even though they might remain invisible or anonymous. Section 1.8 looks at text producers and other participants in further detail.

For most texts, there is no 'one' audience or text receiver: meanings are likely to be different for different people. The audience for Text 1A is fairly specific, and aims to capture the attention of people locking up their bicycle (rather than people interested in linguistics). The text seems quite confident in its message: phrases like 'do not attach' and 'they will cause damage' are fairly unambiguous, in that it is clear how the text producer wants its readers to behave. It's slightly less certain about the likelihood of your bicycle being removed (it tells us they 'may be removed' rather than 'will be removed'), but that doesn't mean it's not a possibility. These phrases are examples of modality, which we will return to in Chapter 4.

KEY TERMS

Text producer: the person or people responsible (through writing and speaking) for creating a text

Text receiver: the person or people interpreting (through reading or listening to) a text

Modality: a system of meaning related to a speaker's attitude to, confidence in, or perception about something in the world

Finally, the text is anchored to a particular time (the time of reading, presumably pre-locking up a bike) and place (Cambridge). If I took the sign and put it on my kitchen wall, it would arguably mean nothing at all, or mean something very different (such as 'the person who placed me here is a sign thief, with a particular liking for signs that protect historic railings'). Either way, the change in context would drastically affect the meaning. It is the language of the text that anchors it to its time and space parameters, with words such as 'these', 'there' and 'opposite'. These words only make the text producer's intended sense in the original context, where they 'point to' the railings and the bicycle rack. If you take the text to my kitchen, where there are neither railings nor bicycle racks, the words no longer point to anything, and are meaningless. The meanings of lots of words are context-dependent like this, and these ones in particular are examples of deixis, which we will return to in Chapter 4.

1.5 Register

When creating a text, a text producer will make their language choices appropriate for the context. In doing so, they are showing awareness of register. Register is determined by its situation of use (context and discourse), as well as by generic conventions (the typical and expected linguistic and structural characteristics of a genre). So, for example, the language used between an employer and an employee in an office is likely to use a different register to a conversation on social media between two friends. Spoken language in the workplace might involve a specific occupational register: for example, it will incorporate words taken from the field of work, and might use more formal grammatical structures; the relationship between participants is perhaps one based on work, rather than a social or personal function. Contextual parameters motivate people to draw on different registers, and we also have expectations and assumptions that others will stick to these 'rules'. We have touched on some aspects of register in our discussion of Text 1A – it's a fairly formal text with an instructive message. Compare this with Text 1B, a note on the front door of a house in Sheffield, UK.

Text 1B

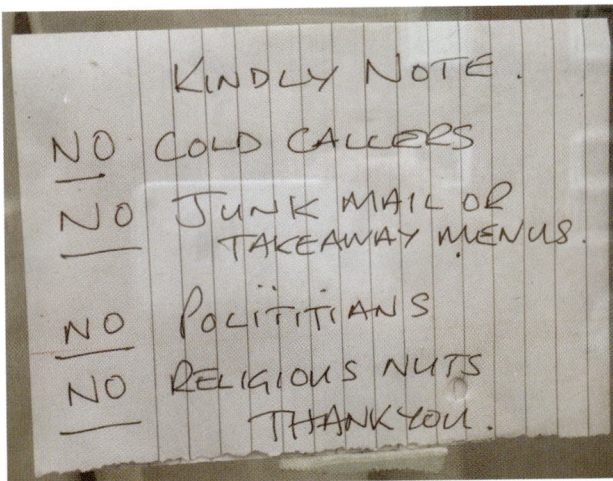

7

KEY TERMS

Register: a variety of language that is associated with a particular situation of use

Genre: a way of grouping texts together based on expected shared conventions

Text 1B shares some similarities with Text 1A: its purpose is to keep people from performing an activity, and it is a public text with a potentially unlimited number of text receivers, though it is directed at four specific groups (cold callers, people who distribute junk mail/takeaway menus, politicians and 'religious nuts'). However, the text producer's motivation for creating the text stems from a different reason of (presumably) having unwanted people knock on their door. Although it uses politeness markers ('kindly note'; 'thankyou'), the language feels more 'forceful' through things such as the repeated underlining of 'no', the repetition of short grammatical structures and the potentially offensive reference to 'religious nuts'. It is highly unlikely that an institutional text producer would draw on such a register for fear of offending people and damaging their own public image. For the text producer of Text 1B however, the text appears on their own property, and many would claim this allows for a more liberal licence in how they use language.

1.5.1 Formality

Formality is a key aspect of register, and it is important to remember that texts don't always fall easily into 'formal' or 'informal' categories. Instead, it's more accurate to think about formality existing on a cline:

Figure 1.1: Formality cline

informal   formal

KEY TERM

Cline: a continuum used in linguistics to indicate a range of a particular language feature: formality, literariness, mode, etc.

ACTIVITY 1.1

The formality cline

Flip forward through the rest of this chapter – place all ten texts in this chapter on the formality cline. Think about how language is shaped by discourse and context, and justify your decisions by making reference to this. You could also collect five texts of your own, and do the same for each of these.

1.6 What is a text?

Throughout this book, the term 'text' is used in a very broad sense. Written and printed texts such as shopping lists, notes, books and newspaper articles are 'texts', but so too are transcripts of spoken language, as well as digital texts such as TV programmes and websites. Any instance of language in use is a text – from a street sign to a novel. This book, which you are reading now, is a text. It has its own contextual parameters, just like any other text. It falls into a genre, has a specific purpose, and has been created with a certain audience in mind. As a result, the language is shaped in a certain way and uses a specific register. As I type, I am making conscious choices about language – editing, removing and replacing words, and considering the subsequent reader and the reading process as I do so. It is not automatic or spontaneous: it is highly planned and structured. When I finish my work for the day after finishing this chapter, I will use language in a very different way, because of the subsequent change in context. But texts don't just 'mean' by themselves – they need readers or hearers to make meanings from them. Reader response theories argue that the meaning of a text is an *interactive* process between the text and the reader, and at a more distant level, the author. Different people will interpret language in different ways, because of their own beliefs, attitudes and values. They bring their own unique background knowledge and experiences to a text, which combines with linguistic content to create meaning.

Norman Fairclough (2003) refers to texts as 'social events' that can have causal effects – meaning that they have the potential to bring about changes in our knowledge, our beliefs, our attitudes, and our values. They can also bring about more material causal effects, such as persuading us to do things (e.g. an advert can cause us to spend money on a product), or disempower and empower us (e.g. a criminal record or a job offer). They can also start wars, and impose laws, and change a person's status and identity (for example, a marriage certificate, a contract, a change of name, or a medical diagnosis). Of course, a text by itself doesn't do this: they all have text producers and discourses behind them, with various motivations and intentions of their own.

1.7 Using metalanguage

Every subject has its own vocabulary, and linguistics is no different. Metalanguage is language about language: the language that we use to describe language itself. All of you will be familiar with some metalanguage already – words such as 'sentence, 'grammar', and 'word' are fairly 'public' examples. However, doing text analysis requires knowledge of some more technical terms, many of which will be introduced and used throughout this book. Metalanguage is used by linguists because it provides a universally understood set of terms, allowing for the more precise and descriptive ways of talking about language. It is not there to confuse or to exclude, nor is it there to be used to simply try and impress people! Text analysis is about using technical terminology to support and develop interpretations, allowing for more systematic and rigorous insights into how language works. It is not about using terms to simply label parts and pick out linguistic features without discussing their relevance. Although you should use metalanguage in your analysis, it should not get in the way of the ultimate aim of text analysis: exploring how meanings are made. One nice thing about metalanguage is that you can choose the level of detail you wish to go into. For example, consider how the word 'dream' can be classified using a range of terms, each with a higher degree of specificity:

word ⟶ noun ⟶ countable noun ⟶ abstract countable noun

The word 'dream' can be a single word but it is also the name of a thing (noun), which can take a plural form (countable noun) and is an experience (abstract).

KEY TERM

Metalanguage: language about language

1.8 Participants in discourse

Texts exist in a particular context, and require at least two participants for them to 'operate': a text producer and a text receiver. Sometimes it is clear who these people are (as is the case for Text 1C), but that is not always the case. Texts can have a private or a public audience, and can be produced for either individuals or groups. The relationship between participants is an important one, as it influences the language choices in a text. When communicating, participants can either share the same physical context (as in a face-to-face conversation) or they can be separated in time and/or space (such as an email exchange). We call this a split discourse, as is the case for Text 1C. This has important consequences for language and meaning.

> **KEY TERMS**
>
> **Participants:** the text producer(s) and text receiver(s) involved in a given discourse event
>
> **Split discourse:** where communicating participants are separated in time and/or space (for example, an email exchange, a postcard, a phone call, a text message, a book, an advert)

Text 1C

Konichiwa Ian and Chira
I am sending you zen and
love from Japan! It's
everything I dreamed of
and more. I already
want to come back, feel
like I've barely skimmed
the surface. I've eaten some
strange things though... once
is enough for those!

Much love, Lynda xxx

Ian + Chira
12 Private Road
England
UNITED KINGDOM

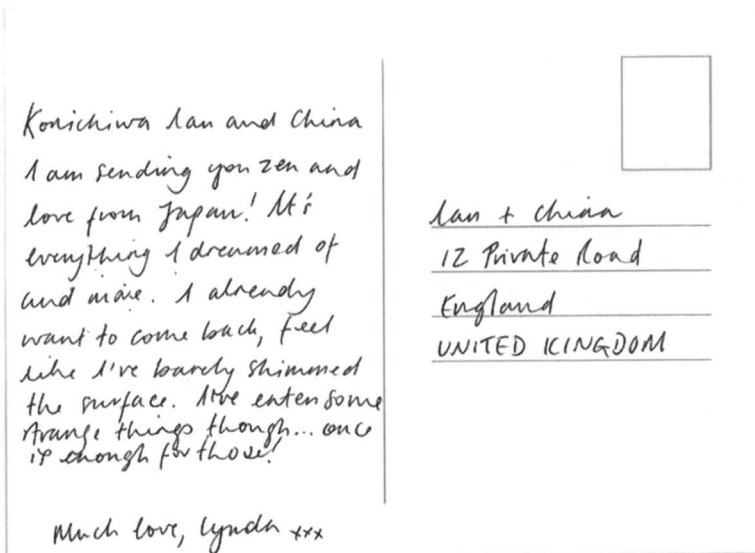

1.8.1 Text producers

A text producer is the person, people or institution responsible (through writing and speaking) for creating a text. Sometimes it is very clear who the text producer is, as in Text 1C. This is a private postcard, created by an individual text producer and directed towards specific text receivers. This is what we would expect to see for such a genre: postcards, and other such private and personal texts like this, create meaning because of the close social proximity between participants. As a result, the register is fairly informal and the text conforms to our typical expectations of this genre: features such as a personal address, a greeting, a sign-off and lists of information about the holiday. The text producer has a very specific motivation in creating the text: to share information about her holiday in Japan.

Sometimes the text producer's identity is not explicitly marked, intentionally masked, anonymous, or not discernible from a text. For example, Text 1D is a note that I left in my kitchen for some friends who were staying over. The text producer's identity is not explicitly marked in the text because there is no need for it to be: although it's a personal text, directed at specific text receivers, they don't need to be told who the text producer is, because of the context in which they are going to read it.

Text 1D

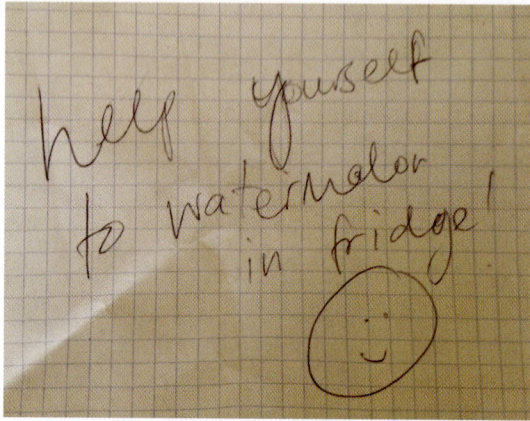

Whereas Texts 1C and 1D both have clearly defined actual writers (the 'real' person responsible for text production), Text 1E is different. This is part of a digital receipt for purchasing train tickets online. Although it obviously must have an actual writer, the identity of this person is unknown: it has an implied writer. In this case, the implied writer is seemingly someone who represents the train company, has a thorough knowledge of the train service, and is able to pass on reliable information to the text receiver. What makes this text even more interesting is that the implied writer takes on the role of the reader too, in asking questions, using the first person 'I'. This is an example of audience positioning, where, in this instance, the reader becomes part of the text, and hopefully accepts the information being given to them.

Text 1E

FAQs

Q: What happens if I don't have the card I booked with/or a new card?

A: You will need to phone our After Sales Support team before arriving at the station on 0344 556 5650 quoting your booking reference.

Q: When should I arrive at the station?

A: Always allow plenty of time to get to the station, collect your ticket(s), check the platform your train is departing from and board the train. At London Euston the train doors close 2 minutes before departure, so please leave plenty of time to get on the train.

KEY TERMS

Social proximity: the perceived remoteness between participants and groups – for example, a married couple have a very narrow social distance, whereas a shop keeper and a customer have a wide social distance

Actual writer: the real person or people responsible for text production

Implied writer: the authorial presence projected by a specific narrative

Audience positioning: how different audiences are targeted by text producers, which results in different interpretations of a text

1.8.2 Text receivers

As mentioned in section 1.6, the text receiver is an integral part of the meaning-making process. People engaged in a discourse event do not merely absorb language passively – reading and listening is a highly active and creative process. To highlight the nature of text receiver creativity, try out Activity 1.2.

ACTIVITY 1.2

Creating mental images and text-worlds

Read Text 1F. As you do so, consciously reflect on the mental image (or text-world) that is created in your mind. What kind of individual memories, knowledge and experience are you using to do this? Compare your text-world with somebody else's. What is the same or different? Discuss why this might be the case.

Text 1F

The beach splits into two, with a strand either side of the waterfront seventeenth-century Forte do Santiago (now a police office); offshore, jet skis and little ketches zip up and down the clear blue sea. A Moorish castle sits above Sesimbra, a stiff half-hour climb from the centre. Within the walls are a church and various ruins, while a circuit of battlements gives amazing panoramas over the surrounding countryside and coastline.

Extract from *Rough Guide to Portugal* (2000)

> **KEY TERM**
>
> **Text-world:** a conceptual representation (or mental image) of language that is created by linguistic content and individual knowledge

1.8.3 Audience positioning

The sociologist Stuart Hall (1973) has been particularly influential in trying to identify the ways in which audiences might be positioned to read and interpret texts in particular ways. His 'encoding/decoding' model of communication is a method of text analysis that focuses on how texts are produced, distributed and interpreted. He suggests that all texts are encoded with certain meanings, which are informed by the text producer/receiver's own cultural background and world-view, and the way that audiences are positioned. This means then, that texts can carry multiple meanings (known as polysemy) when they are decoded by a text receiver. He proposed three ways that audiences are positioned to decode texts:

- **Dominant-hegemonic reading**: the text receiver fully accepts the text in the way that the text producer intended. There is no misunderstanding between the producer and receiver, because they share the same cultural background and world-view. For example: a private postcard between two close friends.

- **Negotiated position**: the text receiver acknowledges and understands the dominant-hegemonic reading, and may broadly accept this, but decodes the text in a way that is different to the text producer's intentions. Text receivers therefore *negotiate* the meaning of a text in line with their own cultural background and world-view. For example: an advert for a product that the text receiver doesn't necessarily need, but understands why others might.

- **Oppositional position**: the text receiver understands the intended meaning of a text, but ultimately rejects it. For example: an argument between two politicians from radically different parties, or somebody who rejected the apparent 'power' of the sign in Text 1A and locked their bicycle to the railings.

The way that text receivers interpret texts is also affected by other contextual variables such as their mood, age, gender, occupation, and so on – meaning that text receivers play a role in positioning *themselves* in the interpretation of texts.

> **KEY TERM**
>
> **Polysemy:** where words, phrases or texts have many possible meanings, often as a result of the text producer/receiver's cultural background and world-view

1.8.4 Discourse communities

So far we have been talking about text producers and receivers mainly in isolation: individuals who create and interpret texts on their own. But texts of course do not just have individual readers and writers. Instead, participants in discourse are members of a discourse community, a term developed by the linguist John Swales. A discourse community is a group of people involved in and communicating about a particular topic or issue. The members are likely to interpret texts in shared ways, based on shared values, world-views and mutual communicative goals. For example, a group of undergraduate English students are members of the same discourse community: they discuss things related to the study of English, they have a mutual goal of learning about language and literature, and they know that certain things can and cannot be said within the context of their community. Each member of this discourse community will be a member of various others, which may or may not cross over with one another. So, imagine a person who is a member of the undergraduate English students' discourse community during the week. At the weekend they switch to a different discourse community when they leave university and go to play the drums in a heavy metal band. People are likely to behave and use language differently according to the discourse community they are currently operating in – an undergraduate English student may discuss complex grammatical concepts and the latest assignment, but are fairly unlikely to do the same thing when operating in a heavy metal discourse community. Language use in a particular discourse community is governed by explicit/implicit rules, social conventions and expectations, and membership of a discourse community is only permitted if these are adhered to.

KEY TERM

Discourse community: a group of people involved in and communicating about a particular topic or issue, that typically share values, world-views and ways of using language

ACTIVITY 1.3

Your own discourse communities

List all the discourse communities you are a member of. What expectations and 'rules' (either explicit or implicit) do each of these have? Where do the boundaries lie? Are there crossovers? How is language typically used across each of these? Are there any words or phrases that belong to each discourse community? For example, English teachers might talk about 'past tense verbs', 'Shakespearean sonnets' and 'semantics', but a discourse community of professional golfers are unlikely to!

1.9 Language as a system of meaning

Language is a fairly efficient human communicative tool, but it is far from perfect. Misunderstandings, double meanings and failures to communicate an intended message are all results of imperfections in language. Constructing meanings is about the potential effects of language choices on a text receiver (for example, choosing a certain level of formality to address a listener, or a word with particular connotations to mean different things to readers).

1.9.1 How are meanings made?

Charles Ogden's and Ivor Richards' (1923) 'triangle of meaning' is a useful way to consider how meanings are made. This is a model of communication that shows the relationship between a 'thought', a 'symbol' and a 'referent'. In this model, the thought is held by an individual; the symbol is a word that represents the thought; the referent is the object or idea in the world to which the symbol points to. Figure 1.2 illustrates this relationship, and the indirect link between symbol and referent. Imagine two participants, Andrew and Danya, who have both been thinking about getting a dog. They use the same symbol, *dog*, to communicate this thought. However, unbeknown to them, their referents in the real world are different: Andrew is thinking of a labradoodle; Danya is thinking of a golden retriever. In this case, the symbol *dog* doesn't point to one specific object in the world: it is *representative* of a group of objects.

Figure 1.2: Triangle of meaning

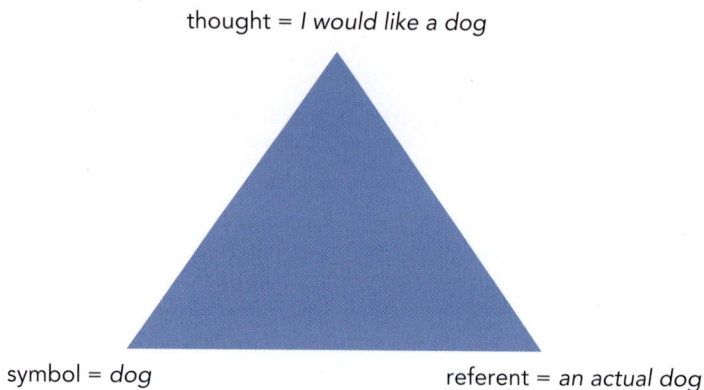

thought = *I would like a dog*

symbol = *dog*   referent = *an actual dog*

In this example, language is inadequate in that it fails to serve as a fully effective communicative tool. The relationships between symbols and referents is therefore arbitrary: they have no meaning until language users assign one to them in a given context. Not all texts work like this, however. A no-smoking sign is non-arbitrary because the meaning is contained within its form. Chapter 3 will explore how meanings are made in more detail.

1.9.2 Representation

We can use language to represent thoughts and ideas, and communicate those thoughts and ideas to somebody else. Representation is an important concept in exploring how text producers present ways of creating meaning and viewing the world. However, with language, we often have multiple ways of representing the same thing, known as construal. Constructing representations is about how language is used to convey a particular set of ideas about an event, process, group of people, etc. (for example, looking at how language choices construct a representation of young people as lazy and difficult, or represent an event such as a protest from one side rather than another). The *re-* in representation is particularly important, as it highlights the fact that the presentation of something is often mediated through somebody else; or, is filtered through someone else's view of the world. This is true of individual words, where a word (such as 'dog') is symbolic and only 'points to' a physical object in the world, and texts are made up of words that represent different people, places and events. Representation then, is tied up with the notion of discourse and is inherently ideological. Paul Baker defines it as the following: 'the creation of a mental image of something using signifying practices and symbolic systems (i.e. through language)' (2014: 73).

KEY TERMS

Construal: the ability that language has to represent/perceive the same thing in different ways

Representation: the portrayal of events, people and circumstances through language and other meaning-making resources (e.g. images and sound) to create a way of seeing the world

---

Text 1G is a 2008 cover of *Men's Health*, a popular UK men's magazine. It provides an interesting example of how men are represented. This has an institutional text producer, and might be said to project fairly stereotypical representations of male behaviour and interests: money, fitness, power, sexual relationships and sport.

- **Layout and images**: Barack Obama, the US president at the time, is foregrounded in the centre of the cover, attracting our attention and looking directly into the camera. He is smiling and looks relaxed – note the loose tie and undone top button. His position as US president symbolises power and authority, and the overall composition of the image appears to be saying 'you can be powerful, respected and wealthy at the same time as being relaxed, stress free and approachable'. This is an attitude that the magazine is trying to project onto its readers, most of which will be from developed countries in the West, where such attitudes are commonplace. The dominant colours of black and red connote importance, seriousness and authority.

Text 1G

- **Lifestyle choices**: the language is taken from specific registers and semantic fields of wealth, authority and power ('special wealth & power issue'; '11 secret money strategies'; 'what great leaders know'); and fitness and appearance ('strong & fit'; '1,785 best ever health, fitness, sex, style & nutrition tips'; '20 heroes of health & fitness'; 'trim the fat in just days'; '15 flat-belly powerfoods').

- **Values and world-views**: men are represented as a discourse community who have shared values and world-views. They are required to be interested in looking good, eating nutritional food, not being overweight, having powerful jobs and earning high salaries – but doing all of this without feeling stressed. Generally, dedicated readers of this magazine will adopt a dominant-hegemonic position, and will 'buy in' to the representation of the world and 'maleness' that is projected here.

KEY TERM

Semantic field: groups of words that relate to a set of meanings for a particular topic

ACTIVITY 1.4
Comparing representations of men

Look at Text 1H, an advert for the 'Campaign Against Living Miserably', a charity that seeks to prevent male suicide by encouraging men to talk about their feelings and problems. Consider the representation of males in this text, comparing it against the kinds of world-views that are projected in Text 1G. What kind of male discourses and representations is the text suggesting? How does this sit alongside your own world-view of male discourses, and how are you positioned as a reader? What kind of reading do you take, according to the encoding/decoding model of communication?

Text 1H

1.10 Mode and genre

We'll now move on to explore two important concepts: mode and genre.

1.10.1 Mode

Language is usually either written or spoken (it is also a system of gestures, as with facial expressions, body language and sign language). Speech and writing are known as modes of communication, and they clearly have some differences, as outlined in Table 1.1. This way of categorising texts is known as the oppositional view.

KEY TERM

Mode: a meaning-making system or channel of human communication

Text Analysis and Representation

Table 1.1: Speech and writing (adapted from Crystal, 2006)

Spoken mode	Written mode
Time-bound, dynamic, non-permanent. Both participants usually present.	Space-bound, static, permanent. Often participants share a split-discourse.
Usually spontaneous. Sentence boundaries often unclear.	Allows the text producer to plan and edit language. Structural units (sentences, paragraphs) are usually easy to identify.
Participants can rely on contextual cues such as body language and facial expressions as an additional communication channel, as well as deixis (e.g. *here, now, that, these*).	Participants cannot always rely on the immediate context to make meanings clear.
Uses sounds for prosodic variation (volume, tone, pitch, intonation, rhythm).	Prosodic variation is limited to punctuation (e.g. capitals for shouting; question marks for rising pitch at the end of questions).
Usually informal and grammatically simple.	Usually formal and grammatically complex.
Very suited to social contexts where casual or unplanned conversation is desirable.	Very suited to the recording of facts and communication of ideas, and to tasks related to memory and learning.

Although the oppositional view is a good starting point, many texts do not fall easily into this kind of distinction. A more nuanced way of looking at mode then, is to consider a speech–writing cline (see Figure 1.3), which allows for blended-mode texts. Consider Text 1I, which is part of a WhatsApp conversation between two participants. This clearly has some elements of writing (is permanent, allows the text producer to edit) and some elements of speaking (is an immediate form of communication, is informal, has a social function).

KEY TERM

Blended-mode: a text which contains conventional elements of both speech and writing

Text 1I

On the speech–writing cline then, we would probably place Text 1I somewhere in the middle:

Figure 1.3: The speech–writing cline

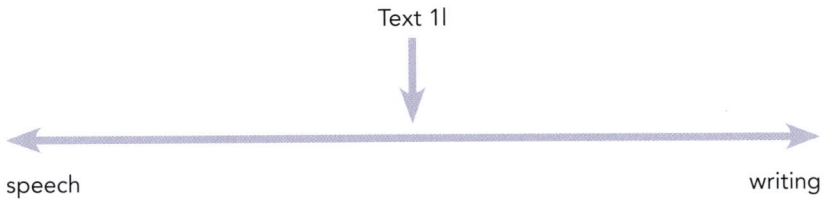

Text 1I

speech   writing

1.10.2 Genre

Texts are further classifiable by the genre that they fall into. Different genres have typical linguistic features and characteristics. For example, the genre of food writing would typically include: a set of recipes grouped by style of cooking, region or food type; information about ingredients and methods; instructions on how to prepare a range of meals; images, and so on.

As is the case for mode, texts do not always fit neatly into a single category. Take for example, Text 1J, which is an extract from *The Kitchen Diaries* by Nigel Slater. In this, the text producer draws on the food writing and diary genres to create a text that relies heavily on intertextuality. The resulting effect is one of intimate, private writing (a typical feature of the diary genre) that is shared with a mass audience and has an instructional purpose (a typical feature of the food writing genre).

KEY TERM

Intertextuality: a process by which texts borrow from or refer to conventions of other texts for a specific purpose and effect

Text 1J

January 4

A salad of cabbage and bacon

Supper is a tightwad affair of shredded cabbage, steamed till just bright and almost tender, tossed with shredded bacon slices and their hot fat spiked with a dash of white wine vinegar. What lifts this from the mundane is the fact that I keep the cabbage jewel bright and use the best, lightly smoked bacon in generous amounts. A few caraway seeds add a nutty, almost musky flavour. Not the sort of things to serve guests but fine for a weekday supper.

Extract from *The Kitchen Diaries*, Nigel Slater (2011)

ACTIVITY 1.5

Recreating genre

In no more than 200 words, rewrite Text 1J removing the intertextual connections, so that it fits neatly into either the food writing genre or the diary genre. Or, you could rewrite it to include more intertextual links – for example, making it into a radio script, a poem, a love letter, a menu, etc. Once you have finished, provide a short analysis of your own writing, explaining your linguistic choices and how you have manipulated generic conventions and intertextual connections to create a new text.

1.11 Purpose

All texts have a purpose, which can be inferred from thinking about participants' motivations in being involved in a discourse event. The majority of texts are multi-purpose in that they do a number of things at the same time: they can *inform* audiences about new information, *persuade* them to buy things or believe in an idea, *explain* the reasons behind decisions, *advise* them on what to do or think, or *describe* a place, memory, event or person, and so on. Looking again at Text 1J, we can say that it holds multiple purposes or functions, because of the text producer's motivations. The primary purpose is probably to *instruct* text receivers on how to make a cabbage and bacon salad, and readers would expect this kind of purpose from such a genre of writing – even though typical imperative structures of this genre, such as 'steam the cabbage' and 'fry the bacon' are nowhere to be found. However, it also has a secondary purpose to 'inform' and 'entertain': it is written in a personal style, uses the first person 'I' to create a familiar, intimate narrative, and 'borrows' from the generic conventions of a diary to allow the readers an insight into the private life of the text producer. An even further purpose might be to *persuade* readers to try the recipe for themselves, and continue reading the rest of the book.

1.12 Approaches to analysing texts

The final section of this chapter will explore some of the ways that texts are analysed, setting out some key principles and approaches to doing this kind of linguistics.

1.12.1 Everyday linguistics: noticing real language

All of the texts looked at so far have been authentic examples of language, taken from my own observations and interactions. Good text analysis is concerned with how language works in real contexts, rather than inventing sentences to exemplify or demonstrate a particular point. Texts are everywhere: a toothpaste label, a TV news report, a sports commentary, a train ticket – all are genuine instances of language that provide opportunities for analysis. Some texts are certainly more 'interesting' than others, but every text has something about it that can be analysed. Try and become more aware and observant of texts around you, thinking about some of the big issues we have explored here: discourse, context, meaning, representation and participants.

1.12.2 Describing, not prescribing

In analysing texts, you should adopt a descriptive rather than a prescriptive approach. Whereas a prescriptive approach is concerned with hierarchical notions of linguistic standards, correctness and rules, descriptive linguistics is concerned with exploring, analysing and describing language in context. This draws attention to how language is actually used in society, and celebrates linguistic diversity. For example, a prescriptivist would argue that certain accents are 'better' than others, that we should try and stop languages changing, and that regional varieties of language are a sub-class of a 'standard' language. In her 1995 book *Verbal Hygiene*, Deborah Cameron suggests that prescriptivism is essentially 'linguistic purism', or 'discourses and practices through which people attempt to "clean up" language and make its structure or its use conform more closely to their ideas of beauty, truth, efficiency, logic, correctness and civility'.

KEY TERMS

Prescriptivism: a view of language that is concerned with standards and correctness

Descriptivism: a view of language that is concerned with describing language in use

1.12.3 What does good text analysis look like?

Text analysis then, is not only the analysis of words or sounds: it also includes what Norman Fairclough (2000) calls 'interdiscursive analysis': seeing texts in terms of the different discourses, genres and styles they draw upon and articulate together. These 'bigger' concepts of discourse and context are brought together with smaller-scale language features: lexis and semantics, pragmatics, grammar, phonetics/phonology/prosodics and graphology, which will be explored in the following chapters. One effective method of textual analysis consists of finding connections between smaller-scale language features and larger-scale related to discourse and context. Rob Pope (1995) argues that all language analysis is a form of creativity, and that interpreting a text requires the text producer to *re-create* it for themselves, as you did in Activity 1.5.

RESEARCH QUESTION

Noticing language and engaging in discourse

Find ten short texts (written and spoken) from your everyday experience, and answer the following questions for each one:

- What kind of world-views and discourses are inherent in the text itself? How do you know?

- Who are the participants? What kind of relationship exists between them? What kind of discourse communities might be involved, and how do you know?

- Summarise the meaning of each text as simply as possible. Can you capture this in a single sentence? A single word? An image?

- How are you positioned as a reader? Do you adopt a dominant-hegemonic, negotiated position or oppositional position?

- What genre(s) are involved? Can you find any examples of intertextuality, and if so, what might be the reasons for this?

- Can you place them on a speech–writing cline and justify your reasons?

Now try and group the texts together in as many different ways as you can. For example, you could group them together based on purpose, formality or discourse community. Give reasons for your groupings. Can you create any sub-groups within your initial groups? Is there any way to categorise all the texts together in a single group?

Wider reading

Read more about text analysis and the nature of studying language by exploring the following books:

English, F. and Marr, T. (2015) *Why Do Linguistics?* London: Bloomsbury.

Fromkin, V., Rodman, R. and Hyams, N. (2013) *An Introduction to Language*. Boston: Wadsworth.

Yule, G. (2015) *The Study of Language* (Sixth edition). Cambridge: Cambridge University Press.

Chapter 2
The structure of
language: building words

In this chapter you will:

- Explore the phonological and lexical features of
  the English language

- Consider how phonological and lexical features
  create meaning

- Apply this knowledge to text analysis

In the next two chapters, we turn our attention to the lexical (word) and grammatical (structural) system of language.

2.1 How language is organised

Language can be broken down into a series of small parts that can each be analysed separately. We will work through these levels of language in turn; however, it is important to remember that text analysis is concerned with how these smaller parts work together as a whole unit. This is known as a systemic analysis of language, and includes those things 'above' the level of the sentence (discourse and context) as well as actual textual elements (sounds, words and grammar). Systemic analyses often use a non-hierarchical rank scale, which shows how smaller units of language are built up to create larger ones:

phoneme ➞ morpheme ➞ word ➞ phrase ➞ clause ➞ sentence ➞ text

The next two chapters are organised in the same way as the rank scale, moving through each level of language in turn. The levels do not necessarily reflect the way we read texts, but they can certainly be a useful 'way in' to analysing texts. You might analyse each level in turn, but there is certainly no requirement to do this – do what works best for you!

KEY TERM

Rank scale: a way of showing how smaller units of language are built up to create larger ones

2.2 Phonetics and phonology

Phonetics and phonology are concerned with the sounds of language: individual vowels and consonants, varieties of speech sounds across individuals and social groups, how speech sounds change over time, accents and dialects, and prosody (rhythm, intonation and stress patterns). Phonetics is the production and perception of speech sounds, whereas phonology refers to the systems of sounds used in different languages. The study of phonetics and phonology is important for the analysis of all modes of language, not just spoken texts.

2.2.1 Describing sounds

A very useful tool for describing spoken language is the phonetic alphabet, a system designed by linguists to record different speech sounds in an accurate and systematic manner. Discrete speech sounds are known as phonemes and each of these sounds has its own symbol in the alphabet. English has around 44 phonemes (depending on your accent), which are shown in Table 2.1. The underlined part of each word corresponds to the phonetic symbol on the left.

Table 2.1: The sounds of English

Consonants		Vowels	
p	pip	Short vowels	
b	bib	ɪ	pit
t	ten	e	pet
d	den	æ	pat
k	cat	ɒ	pot
ɡ	get	ʌ	but
f	fish	ʊ	book
v	voice	ə	mother
θ	thigh	Long vowels	
ð	this	iː	bean
s	set	ɜː	burn
z	zoo	ɑː	barn
ʃ	ship	ɔː	born
ʒ	measure	uː	boon

Consonants		Vowels	
h	hen	**Diphthongs**	
tʃ	church	aɪ	bite
ʤ	judge	eɪ	bait
m	man	ɔɪ	boy
n	now	əʊ	toe
ŋ	sing	aʊ	house
l	let	ʊə	cure
r	ride	ɪə	ear
w	wet	eə	air
j	yet		

In spoken language, phonemes are strung together in a continuous stream of air, which can then be transcribed using the phonetic alphabet. Slash brackets are used to indicate this, as in the following examples:

dog	/dɒg/
measure	/meʒə/
computer	/kɒmpju:tə/
grass	/grɑ:s/

Note that for 'grass', the transcription uses the long /ɑ:/ vowel, reflecting a southern English accent. For northern English, the short /æ/ vowel is used in this position, to give /græs/. There are plenty of other examples of regional and global variation in accents, and a speaker's accent forms a large part of their sociolinguistic identity.

KEY TERM

Accent: variation in pronunciation associated with a particular geographical region

---

ACTIVITY 2.1

Using the phonetic alphabet

Transcribe your full name, hometown and age using the phonetic alphabet. Remember you are interested in sounds rather than spelling, and that the transcription should match your own accent. Next, transcribe the following words: *television, knife, password, charge, thumb*. Compare with a partner. Were there any differences in your transcriptions that could be a result of people's accents?

2.2.2 The mechanics of speech

Speech production is a highly dynamic affair, involving various combinations of movements by the vocal articulators and their interaction with airflow. Figure 2.1 shows the vocal tract and the different vocal articulators involved in the production of speech.

KEY TERM

Vocal articulator: a different part of the vocal tract involved in the production of speech sounds (e.g. lips, tongue, alveolar ridge, vocal folds)

Figure 2.1: The vocal tract

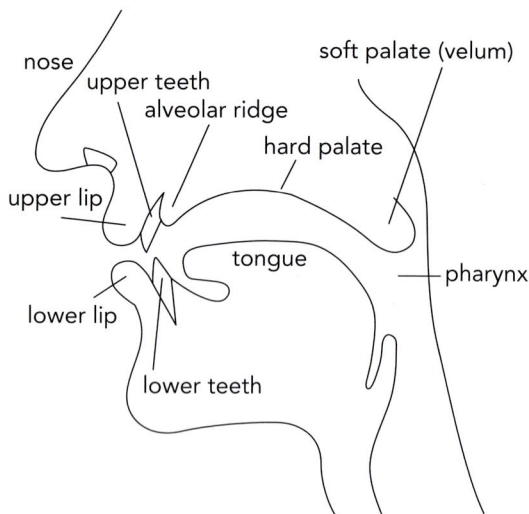

2.2.2.1 Vowels

In producing vowels, air is pushed from the lungs and out through the mouth and/or nose. They can be short, long, or diphthongs, which is where a speaker glides from one vowel sound to another.

> **KEY TERM**
>
> **Diphthong:** a vowel sound that is the combination of two separate sounds, where a speaker moves from one to another

2.2.2.2 Consonants

Consonants are defined by three variables:

1   their manner of articulation

2   their place of articulation

3   voicing, which is whether the sound is voiced (with vocal vibration) or voiceless (without vocal fold vibration).

> **KEY TERM**
>
> **Voicing:** the vibration of the vocal folds in the production of speech. Voiced sounds are those made with vibration; unvoiced sounds are those without vibration.

Their distribution is shown in Table 2.2 where in each cell, unvoiced sounds are on the left and voiced sounds are on the right:

Table 2.2: English consonants

Manner of articulation	Place of articulation							
	Bilabial	Labiodental	Dental	Alveolar	Post-alveolar	Palatal	Velar	Glottal
Plosive	p b			t d			k g	
Nasal	m			n			ŋ	
Fricative		f v	θ ð	s z	ʃ ʒ			h
Affricate					tʃ dʒ			
Approximant	w				r	j		
Lateral				l				

- Plosives are made when two articulators touch each other – for example, the upper and lower lip are held together in the production of /p/. Air pressure builds up behind the articulators and is released in a burst.

- Nasals are similar to plosives in that two articulators are touching, but air is released through the nose.

- Fricatives involve near contact of the articulators, and air is pushed out through a small space.

- Affricates begin as a plosive and end as a fricative.

- Approximants are produced without articulators making contact: not quite as close as fricatives, but further apart than vowels.

- Laterals are produced by articulators making contact and air flowing down the sides of the tongue.

2.2.3 Sound iconicity

Text producers can use particular phonological patterns to create meaning in texts. This is an example of sound iconicity. The sounds are iconic in that they often reflect actions they describe, or point to events and objects in the real world. Brand names often exploit sound iconicity and are a good genre to discuss here. Let's look at two well-known brands, Tic Tac® and Zippo®:

Tic Tac /tɪktæk/

The small size of the mints is reflected in the shortness of the individual speech sounds: repeated plosives (see consonance) that provide bursts of sound on either side of the short vowels.

Zippo /zɪpəʊ/

The word is onomatopoeic: it works on the reader's familiarity with the sound that the product itself (a cigarette lighter) makes in the real world. The voiced fricative /z/ is a maintainable sound, meaning it can last as long as the speaker's breath allows, in the same way that the flame produced from a lighter works.

KEY TERMS

Sound iconicity: the matching of sound to an aspect of meaning

Consonance: a pattern of repeated consonant sounds for effect

Onomatopoeia: words that have some associated meaning between their sound and what they represent

ACTIVITY 2.2
Phonology in poetry
Read Text 2A, an extract taken from the poem 'Digging' by Seamus Heaney. How does he use sound iconicity to evoke the scene being described?

Text 2A

Under my window, a clean rasping sound

When the spade sinks into gravelly ground:

...

The cold smell of potato mould, the squelch and slap

Of soggy peat, the curt cuts of an edge

Extract from 'Digging', Seamus Heaney (2002)

2.3 Grammar: building words

Defining the term 'word' is a surprisingly complex task (try it, and see!). Would you class 'swim' and 'swims' as two different words, for example? In this section, we shall see that building words is a highly productive activity, and there are various ways in which it happens.

2.3.1 The structure of words: morphology

The area of linguistics that deals with the structure of words is called morphology, and the units which make up words are called morphemes. These are best described as the smallest unit of language that can convey meaning, and cannot be broken down into anything further that is meaningful. Many simple words are morphemes by themselves: *elephant*, *child* and *sing*, for example. As a unit, *elephant* has a complete meaning by itself: we don't break it down into *el*, *eph* and *ant*. These then, can be called free morphemes: they can exist in isolation. Sometimes, a word consists of two or more morphemes: we can add an *-s* to create *elephants*, *-ren* to create *children,* and *-ing* to create *singing*. The morphemes *-s*, *-ren* and *-ing* all convey meaning, though they cannot stand alone and must be 'glued' to something else. We call these little bits that glue onto other words bound morphemes.

Bound morphemes can be further categorised depending on where they attach themselves:

- Before the root word, in which case they are prefixes (e.g. <u>pre</u>*determine*; <u>un</u>*clear*; <u>re</u>*fresh*)

- After the root word, in which case they are suffixes (e.g. tall*er*; trees;
  un*usually*). These morphemes are meaningful in that they can express tense
  (*hid* vs. *hidden*), plurality (*cat* vs. *cats*) and possession (*Jane* vs. *Jane's*).

A final, but very rare (in English, at least) type of morpheme is an infix. As you
might expect, this is where a morpheme attaches itself inside another word, such
as *fan-bloody-tastic*.

KEY TERMS

Morphology: the internal structure of words

Morpheme: a unit that makes up a word

Free morpheme: a morpheme that can stand on its own and can
usually form a word in its own right

Bound morpheme: a morpheme that cannot stand on its own

Prefix: a morpheme that appears before a root word to modify
its meaning

Suffix: a morpheme that appears after a root word to modify
its meaning

Infix: a morpheme that appears inside a root word to modify its meaning

---

2.3.1.1 Inflection and derivation

There are two main ways of building words using bound morphemes: inflection
and derivation. Inflectional morphemes do not drastically alter the meaning of a
word, and are added to nouns, verbs and adjectives according to usage. In each
case, the word class remains the same, despite the addition of a morpheme:

- Nouns can inflect to show plurals (*coat* → *coats*)

- Verbs can inflect to show tense (*work* → *works, worked, working*)

- Adjectives can inflect to show comparison (*big* → *bigger* → *biggest*)

KEY TERMS

Inflection: the way that a morpheme shows a grammatical category
such as a verb tense or a plural noun

Derivation: the way that a morpheme helps form a new word

Derivational morphemes have a more dramatic effect on the meaning or category of a root word. Look at the different variations of *clean* in these examples:

1 The trains were *clean* and on time. (adjective, where *clean* describes an appearance)

2 The trains were *unclean* and late. (adjective, where *unclean* describes a very different appearance)

3 He is a *cleaner* for the train company. (noun, where *cleaner* refers to a person)

4 I was *cleaning* the trains all night. (verb, where *cleaning* is a process)

2.3.1.2 Compounding

Words can also be built up of more than one free morpheme. This is known as compounding, and examples include *blackboard*, *skyscraper*, *footpath* and *windmill*. Many compounds are so ingrained into English that you might not even notice them: *breakfast* and *cupboard*, for example.

KEY TERM

Compounding: the formation of a new word from two or more existing words

---

2.4 Categories of words

In any language, words can be divided into word classes, defined by their structural properties and the way they behave in sentences. These categories reflect the way that language is organised. In this section, we will look closely at the nine major word classes of English:

nouns	pronouns	verbs
adjectives	adverbs	prepositions
determiners	conjunctions	interjections

Interjections are words such as *yikes!*, *shhh!* and *yuck!*, and are fairly low in number. We will not say much about them here. The majority of new words entering the language fall into the categories of nouns, verbs, adjectives or adverbs, and therefore these are known as 'open' or lexical word classes. These words are *lexical* in that they carry meaning as an individual word. Categories that don't admit new members are known as 'closed' or grammatical word classes (prepositions, determiners and conjunctions). These words play a *grammatical* or *structural* role, working with other words to build up sentences. We will see that the majority of word classes are broken down into sub-classes, and that many words can fall into multiple categories.

KEY TERMS

Word class: a category (or type) of word that behaves in the same way in a sentence

Noun: a word that names a physical thing or abstract concept

Pronoun: a word that substitutes for a noun phrase

Verb: a word denoting actions, states or events

Adjective: a word that modifies a noun phrase

Adverb: a word that modifies a verb, an adjective or another adverb

Preposition: a word that shows connections between other words, often showing a sense of place or time

Determiner: a word that appears before a noun phrase and helps to give it some definition

Conjunction: a word that connects similar or different units together

Interjection: a word whose function is purely emotive

2.4.1 Nouns

Typically, nouns refer to physical things and abstract concepts. They are one of the most prominent forms of a language and carry meaning by themselves. They point to physical things in the world (*apple, water, Brazil*) and abstract concepts that exist in our minds (*love, democracy, politics*). Nouns signal who or what are involved in texts, and have a role in the creation of description and building rich, fictional worlds. To demonstrate, look at Text 2B, which is the opening to *Dombey and Son* by Charles Dickens (1846):

Text 2B

Dombey sat in the corner of the darkened room in the great arm-chair by the bedside, and Son lay tucked up warm in a little basket bedstead, carefully disposed on a low settee immediately in front of the fire.

Extract from *Dombey and Son*, Charles Dickens

Here, Dickens uses a range of nouns to build a world and create a description for his readers. Proper nouns such as 'Dombey' and 'Son' trigger images of humans (or perhaps animals), and there are plenty of common nouns that are used to create a rather vivid and rich text-world: 'basket bedstead' suggests a brown woven material; 'room' suggests four walls with doors, windows and a ceiling; 'settee' suggests a comfortable chair for more than one person; 'fire' suggests heat and flames, and perhaps other objects such as coal and wood.

You may have noticed that many of the nouns are modified by other words: 'darkened room', 'great arm-chair', 'little basket bedstead' and 'low settee', for example. Words build up in this way to form phrases, and so we can call these chunks of words noun phrases. We will return to a more detailed discussion of phrases in section 3.2, but they are groups of grammatically connected words that have a head word.

KEY TERMS

Phrase: a group of words that is grammatically connected and defined by its head word

Noun phrase: a phrase that has a noun as its head word

Head word: the most important, pivotal word in a phrase

Nouns can be classified into smaller categories, as in Table 2.3:

Table 2.3: Categories of nouns

Sub-category	Description	Examples
Proper noun	Refers to names of people, places and organisations. Always starts with a capital letter.	Istanbul, Monday, University of Manchester, Henry
Concrete noun	Refers to objects that have a physical existence. Can be countable (take a plural) or non-countable (do not take a plural).	**Countable:** chair, school, train
		Non-countable: rice, water, poultry
Abstract noun	Refers to states, feelings and concepts that do not have a physical existence.	love, anger, bravery, trust, change

Politicians are often noted for using abstract nouns in their language, as a method of talking about things that are difficult to define, but in ways that can sound convincing. The following examples are taken from a 2005 speech on education reform by Tony Blair (who was the UK's Prime Minister, at the time). The abstract nouns have been underlined.

> We must do better to tackle the pockets of deep educational <u>disadvantage</u>.

> You can see the <u>progress</u> in the buildings, in the computers and the results.

> They must now become self-sustaining to provide irreversible <u>change</u> for the better.

What do 'disadvantage', 'progress' and 'change' actually mean here? The answer is, not much: they are general and allow the text producer to *appear* committed, without actually committing to anything. Because abstract nouns have no 'physical' description, they potentially mean an infinite number of things. In this speech, Tony Blair doesn't specifically define what he means by 'progress' in the buildings, computers and results – but he still uses it as an argument for educational reform and real political changes.

2.4.2 Pronouns

Pronouns are words such as *she, you, I,* and *it.* We will deal with them here as they are sometimes considered to be a sub-class of nouns, and can substitute for nouns and noun phrases in a sentence. Consider the following sentences, where the pronouns have been underlined:

> Well, FIFA got <u>its</u> wish and Cristiano Ronaldo will grace the greatest show on earth next summer, but <u>they</u>'d better hit the ground running.

> But taking 36 of the 51 matches played at Euro 2016 to eliminate eight teams cannot be right. So <u>that</u> has to be looked at. <u>It</u> meant <u>it</u> was a slow-burner.

In each case, the pronouns stand in place of a full noun phrase. It would sound odd if the writer had chosen to repeat the full noun phrase instead (underlined):

> Well, FIFA got <u>FIFA's</u> wish and Cristiano Ronaldo will grace the greatest show on earth next summer, but <u>FIFA</u> had better hit the ground running.

> But taking 36 of the 51 matches played at Euro 2016 to eliminate eight teams cannot be right. So <u>36 of the 51 matches played at Euro 2016 to eliminate eight teams</u> has to be looked at. <u>36 of the 51 matches played at Euro 2016 to eliminate eight teams</u> meant <u>Euro 2016</u> was a slow-burner.

Most pronouns then, 'point to' or refer to other things in a sentence. The thing that is already specified is known as the antecedent, and the pronoun that refers to this is the anaphor.

Jenny	is studying	linguistics	and	she	loves	it
↑		↑		↑		↑
ANTECEDENT 1		ANTECEDENT 2		ANAPHOR 1		ANAPHOR 2

As in these examples, text producers can use antecedents and anaphors to make language more efficient, economic and manageable, but it can also be exploited in order to hold *back* information about something, or to keep somebody's identity anonymous. Consider the first line from the 1916 war poem 'A Working Party' by Siegfried Sassoon, which describes a soldier's experience of trench warfare:

Three hours ago he blundered up the trench

There is no antecedent here: the pronoun 'he' doesn't pick out any specific individual, and one possible interpretation would be one related to anonymity, to suggest that the soldier no longer has an identity as a result of his war experiences. Pronouns can pick out individuals of course, as in personal messages such as 'Are you going tonight?' And 'Your country needs you'.

There are several different sub-classes of pronoun: personal, indefinite, reflexive, reciprocal, demonstrative, interrogative and relative. Texts may involve a number of different sub-classes of pronoun, and these work together as a pronoun system to create meaning.

KEY TERMS

Antecedent: a linguistic unit from which another unit derives its interpretation

Anaphor: a linguistic unit that is defined by its antecedent

Pronoun system: the way that pronouns (either of the same or different sub-classes) work together to create meaning in a text

- Personal pronouns refer to people and are further categorised according to Table 2.4:

Table 2.4: Personal pronouns

Person	Number	Gender	As subject	As object
First	Singular		I	me
	Plural		we	us
Second	Singular		you	you
	Plural		you	you

Person	Number	Gender	As subject	As object
Third	Singular	Masculine	he	him
		Feminine	she	her
		Neutral	it	it
	Plural		they	they

- Indefinite pronouns do not have an antecedent: they do not stand in place of a noun or noun phrase. They refer to things or notions that are not specific, and are words such as *some, someone, somebody, something, no one, nobody, any, anyone, anything, either, both,* and so on.

- Reflexive pronouns all end in *-self* or *-selves* and as the name suggests, are used to refer to a singular or plural person. They must have an antecedent: *He considered <u>himself</u> to be the best salesman in the company.*

- Reciprocal pronouns express a two-way relationship, such as in *each other* and *one another.* Therefore, they take two (or more) antecedents: *Cristiano Ronaldo and Lionel Messi need <u>each other</u>, insists former boss Carlo Ancelotti.*

- Demonstrative pronouns point out things in time and space. There are four of them in English: *this, that, these* and *those.* In spoken language, they will typically be accompanied with a gesture – you could imagine somebody pointing towards something whilst saying *I want <u>this</u> one, not <u>that</u> one.*

- Interrogative pronouns are used to ask questions: *<u>Who</u> won the match? <u>What</u> time is kick off? <u>Which</u> way is the station?*

- Relative pronouns are used at the start of relative clauses; for example: *The girl <u>who</u> got the highest marks won the prize* (see Chapter 3 for more about relative clauses).

ACTIVITY 2.3

Exploring a pronoun system in a text

Text 2C is an email from a charity to express thanks after receiving a donation. Read the text through and highlight all the different types of pronoun. Why might the text producer have used these pronouns? How is the text receiver positioned through the use of pronouns, and what kind of relationship is built between participants, as a result of the grammatical and lexical choices?

Text 2C

THANK YOU IAN

You're amazing!

| Donation amount: £5 | ✓ Payment confirmed |
| Donation reference: 28S2Q3K5TU1WWW8SS0K0WPT78Q | ✉ Emailed to you |

Now help spread the word...

| Post a message on Facebook and tell your friends about the appeal. | Tweet your support and encourage other people to donate. |

THANK YOU!

You've made a difference

Your donation to the DEC Philippines Typhoon Appeal has been submitted successfully and will soon be helping us to provide food, aid and shelter to all those affected by this disaster.

▸ Find out about other ways to help on our website

Dear Ian,

Thank you for your kind donation.

We just wanted to get in touch to let you know we've received your donation and it's on the way to the people who need it most. The world is a much better place thanks to the generosity of people like you.

Your donation will be used to help people whose lives have been turned into nightmares, and will go towards food, shelter and medical supplies to people who are in desperate need. You are literally, a life saver.

Words cannot describe the devastation caused by natural disasters. But actions speak louder than words, and your kind actions will undoubtedly touch the lives of people who need it most.

Together we can make the world a better place.

Thank you.

2.4.3 Verbs

In general terms, verbs are words denoting actions, states or events. Verbs tell us about the things that nouns (and other word classes, such as pronouns) are involved in. There are various ways of classifying verbs, but one important distinction is between lexical verbs and auxiliary verbs.

2.4.3.1 Lexical verbs

Lexical verbs typically function as the main verb in the sentence and carry semantic weight, in that they mean something (you can check by looking up their definition in a dictionary). The following sentences include examples of lexical verbs (taken from texts in Chapter 1):

Shredded cabbage, <u>steamed</u> till just bright and almost tender

When should I <u>arrive</u> at the station?

It's everything I <u>dreamed</u> of and more.

They take a number of inflections to indicate things such as tense and person, a morphological pattern that is governed by whether they are *regular* or *irregular*, as shown in Table 2.5.

Table 2.5: Verb forms

Base form	Third-person singular present (-s form)	Past tense	Past participle (regular -ed form, or irregular)	Present participle (-ing form)
want	wants	wanted	wanted	wanting
play	plays	played	played	playing
eat	eats	ate	eaten	eating
hit	hits	hit	hit	hitting
sing	sings	sang	sung	singing
think	thinks	thought	thought	thinking

Lexical verbs have a number of different sub-classes, and the ones we shall look at here are related to function and semantics. This means that we are interested in the role they play in conveying different types of meaning. This way of classifying verbs follows a tradition developed by Michael Halliday in the 1960s, which sees verbs as *processes* that unfold in time and are carried out by directly involved participants in different circumstances. There are four main types:

- Material verbs are processes of doing and happening, showing actions and events. They relate to physical events in the world, such as *jump*, *touch* and *fall*.

- Mental verbs are processes of sensing, showing internal processes such as thinking. They relate to inner aspects of our experience, such as *think*, *know* and *wish*.

- Verbal verbs are processes of speech, showing external processes of communicating through speech – for example, *say*, *shout* and *talk*.

- Relational verbs are processes of being and having, showing states of being. They are related to identifying and classifying, such as *is*, *become* and *seem*. You will notice that relational verbs can occur with other verb types, meaning they can function as auxiliaries.

To illustrate this way of classifying verbs, consider Text 2D: an extract from a radio commentary of a football match.

Text 2D

I know what it's like (.) they will be <u>very</u> nervous out there (.) I <u>honestly</u> think it's the biggest game in Liverpool's history (.) this is Xabi Alonso in the centre circle (.) now Dietmar Hamann (.) Hamann back to Alonso (.) Alonso turns to his left and plays it through to Riise on the left side (.) Riise hits it against Cafu (.) Riise puts it back into the box (.) <u>goal</u>! (.) and the captain has delivered a blow to AC Milan

In this text, text producer (radio commentator) and text receiver (radio listener) are separated: only the text producer has the benefit of being able to *see* the game being played, and therefore his job is to successfully convey these events to his distant, radio listeners. He uses a large amount of material verb processes so that the text receiver is able to imagine the game being played out for themselves, as in: '<u>turns</u> to his left', '<u>plays</u> it through', '<u>hits</u> it' and '<u>puts</u> it back'. We also have relational verbs such as 'they will <u>be</u> very nervous' and 'this is Xabi Alonso' to show states of being and who is in possession of the ball, and mental verbs such as 'I <u>know</u> what it's like' and 'I honestly <u>think</u>', which the text producer presumably does to fulfil his role of 'expert' ex-footballer on the commentary team.

2.4.3.2 Auxiliary verbs

Auxiliary verbs support the lexical verb in a sentence. They can be spotted by their position in a sentence (usually before the main verb), and indicate change in time scale, person, or number. There are two types: primary (*to be*, *to have*, *to do*) and modal (*can/could, shall/should, may/might, will/would, must*), which can occur together in the same sentence. The following sentences (also taken from Chapter 1) include an auxiliary verb (underlined) and a main verb (in bold):

I <u>am</u> **sending** you Zen and love from Japan.

Please <u>do</u> not **attach** bicycles to these historic railings.

You <u>will</u> need to **phone** our After Sales Support team.

KEY TERM

Modal verb: an auxiliary verb that joins with a main verb to show the degree of commitment towards an event or person that a speaker holds

---

Modal auxiliary verbs show the degree of commitment towards an event or person, and create meaning by telling us something about the lexical verb. Look at this example from Text 2C, where the modals have been underlined:

Words <u>may</u> not describe the devastation caused by Typhoon Haiyan, but on behalf of all those who <u>will</u> receive aid because of your support, thank you.

Note that here the modal 'may' is negated by 'not' – all modal verbs can be modified in this way. What this text means then, is 'donations are more important and useful than words'. In turn, this may encourage other people to donate money which fulfils one of the aims set out by the text producer in creating the text. Modal verbs (part of a larger system called modality) are an important part of text analysis and we will return to examine them in more detail in Chapter 4.

2.4.4 Adjectives

Adjectives modify noun phrases, and typically refer to qualities or states, giving information about things like shape, size, taste, colour, or opinions like good/bad, pretty/ugly, and so on. They display fairly 'free' syntax in that they can appear before a noun phrase (attributively) or after a noun phrase (predicatively), as shown in Table 2.6.

Table 2.6: Positions of adjective phrases

Attributive	Predicative
The *fierce* teacher	Teachers are *fierce*
An *expensive, filthy, unpleasant* meal	It was *expensive, filthy* and *unpleasant*

Note how adjectives can build up to form adjective phrases, to modify noun phrases in as much detail as is required:

The *fierce, rude, mean, cruel, uncivilised, terrible* teacher

The base form of an adjective can be modified to fit into two sub-classes comparative and superlative, as shown in Table 2.7.

Table 2.7: The morphology of adjectives

Sub-class	Description	Examples
Base	The basic, uninflected form of an adjective	small, green, expensive
Comparative	A form used to compare two instances, either by adding the -er suffix or *more*	smaller, greener, more expensive
Superlative	A form used to express the highest or most extreme of something, either by adding the -est suffix or *most*	smallest, greenest, most expensive

KEY TERM

Adjective phrase: a phrase that has an adjective as its head word

2.4.5 Adverbs

Adverbs are another word class that provide additional information about other words in the sentence, usually about place, time and manner. They modify adjectives, verbs, clauses and other adverbs.

- **Place**: we're going <u>away</u> next summer; I've been living <u>here</u> since January

- **Time**: it'll <u>soon</u> be Christmas; I'm <u>still</u> working

- **Manner**: <u>slowly</u> add the stock to the rice; you'll <u>easily</u> pass your exams

They occur as adverb phrases when the adverb is the head word:

She <u>very clearly</u> gave us the directions.

You can get there <u>fairly quickly</u>.

2.4.6 Prepositions

The majority of prepositions express relationships between things in time and space. They occur before noun phrases or pronouns and include words such as *above, over, after, along, behind, near, inside, to, during*, and so on. The prepositions have been underlined in the following sentences, which are all newspaper headlines:

Inflatable moon causes disruption <u>on</u> the roads <u>of</u> Beijing

Captain throws four men <u>off</u> flight <u>after</u> a row sparked <u>over</u> a pair <u>of</u> Nike trainers

New security guard gets stuck <u>in</u> the back <u>of</u> his own van

Prepositions are important to text producers in that they provide orientational cues for how text receivers 'navigate' texts. To illustrate this, look at the following sentences that are taken from a website that lists walking tours around New York City. The text producer makes extensive use of prepositions (which have all been underlined) in order to position the reader as 'part' of the text. The feeling of reader immersion in the text is initially triggered by the use of the second-person singular pronoun *you* in the opening sentence:

This week, Fodor's takes you <u>on</u> a tour <u>of</u> the best stops—and shops— <u>along</u> Fifth Avenue <u>in</u> New York City

This sentence sets up the time and space parameters, positioning the reader as part of the text and in the city itself. It gradually builds the world of New York by further use of prepositions, as well as proper nouns such as 'Rockefeller Centre' and '5th Avenue':

Start this almost one mile walk <u>at</u> the outdoor plaza <u>of</u> the Rockefeller Centre, located <u>between</u> 49th and 50th streets, just west of 5th Avenue.

And, just as is the case for nouns, adjectives and adverbs, prepositional phrases are formed when a preposition is the head word.

Some weird creatures live <u>under the sea</u>

See you <u>in the morning</u>

> **KEY TERM**
>
> **Prepositional phrase:** a phrase that has a preposition as its head word

2.4.7 Determiners

Determiners form part of a noun phrase, and their job is related to how the noun phrase is used to refer to something in the world. Once again, there are sub-classes: articles, possessives and quantifiers, as shown in Table 2.8.

Table 2.8: Determiners

Sub-class	Description	Examples
Article	A form whose basic role is to mark noun phrases as either *definite* or *indefinite*	Definite: <u>the</u> girl Indefinite: <u>a</u> girl; <u>an</u> apple
Possessive	A form that shows ownership of a noun phrase NB: determiners always precede a noun, but if the possessive word appears without a noun, it is a pronoun	<u>my</u> book <u>our</u> house
Demonstrative	A form that has a 'pointing' function, referencing a noun that is nearby (*this*/*these*) or far away (*that*/*those*)	I want <u>this</u> one <u>That</u> is nicer

Determiners are useful in that they are related to specificity. Compare 'turn left at the shop' with 'turn left at a shop' as a set of directions. The indefinite article wouldn't be particularly useful here, as it doesn't point to anything specific in the world.

2.4.8 Conjunctions

Conjunctions are items that link units together. There are two sub-classes: coordinators and subordinators. The coordinators are *and*, *but*, and *or* and they link units of the same category together: NOUN *and* NOUN, for example:

Arsenal <u>and</u> Tottenham's approach for Mauro Icardi has been confirmed.

The most exciting football is in the Premier League <u>but</u> the best football is in Spain.

Text Analysis and Representation

Subordinators link a clause to some other element. Examples include *when*, *if*, *why*, *although*, *because*, *so* and *how*. We will return to them in Chapter 3.

KEY TERMS

Coordinator: a word that links words, phrases and clauses together where they are equal

Subordinator: a word that links clauses together to show one is dependent on another

---

PRACTICE QUESTION

Text analysis

Text 2E is an extract from an online article about Mumbai, as part of the Lonely Planet guide to India. Analyse how the text uses language to create meanings and representations.

Text 2E

Mumbai is big. It's full of dreamers and hard-labourers, starlets and gangsters, stray dogs and exotic birds, artists and servants and fisherfolk and *crorepatis* (millionaires) and lots and lots of people. It has India's most prolific film industry, some of Asia's biggest slums (as well as the world's most expensive home) and the largest tropical forest in an urban zone. Mumbai is India's financial powerhouse, fashion epicentre and a pulse point of religious tension. It's even evolved its own language, Bambaiyya Hindi, which is a mix of … everything.

If Mumbai is your introduction to India, prepare yourself. The city isn't a threatening place but its furious energy, limited public transport and punishing pollution makes it challenging for visitors. The heart of the city contains some of the grandest colonial-era architecture on the planet but explore a little more and you'll uncover unique bazaars, hidden temples, hipster enclaves and India's premier restaurants and nightlife.

Extract from *Lonely Planet India* (2015)

RESEARCH QUESTION
Words in a text: creating a corpus

Find a text of around 75–100 words. For each word in the text, classify its grammatical category and tabulate this data. What does the resulting data reveal about the make-up of the text? For example, what kinds of verb processes are used, and why might this be? What does the pronoun system suggest about the relationship between participants? What other kinds of lexical patterns are interesting, and might be as a result of choices related to genre, mode or subject? Compare your results with somebody else.

Wider reading

Read more about the structure and categories of words, by exploring the following books and chapters:

Aarts, B. and Haegeman, L. (2006) English Word Classes and Phrases. In B. Aarts and A. McMahon (eds). *The Handbook of English Linguistics*. Oxford: Blackwell.

Börjars, K. and Burridge, K. (2010) *Introducing English Grammar* (Second edition). London: Routledge.

Jackson, H. and Stockwell, P. (2010) *An Introduction to the Nature and Functions of Language* (Second edition). London: Bloomsbury.

Lieber, R. (2015) *Introducing Morphology* (Second edition). Cambridge: Cambridge University Press.

Roach, P. (2009) *English Phonetics and Phonology* (Fourth edition). Cambridge: Cambridge University Press.

Chapter 3
The structure of language: building sentences

In this chapter you will:

- Explore the structural features of the English language

- Consider how structural choices create meaning

- Apply this knowledge to text analysis

The previous chapter dealt with lexis and looked at the semantic and structural features of different categories of words. This is a useful part of text analysis, but whole texts are usually made up of more than individual words. Words work together to create phrases, clauses and sentences, which in turn work together to create whole texts. This chapter will also highlight the difference between grammatical form (word classes, phrases and clauses) and grammatical function (subjects, objects, adverbials and complements).

KEY TERMS

Form: labels given to describe what linguistic units *are* (word classes, phrases and clauses)

Function: labels given to describe what linguistic units *do* (subject, object, adverbial, etc.)

3.1 Distribution

Language is remarkable for many reasons, but one particularly interesting feature is the syntactic behaviour, or distribution of words in a sentence. Words organise themselves into a sentence according to their categories, 'slotting' in to various positions. Consider the following distribution of words in these sentences:

1	2	3	4	5	6	7	8	9	10	11
A	small	waitress	served	the	hungry	children	at		the	terrible	restaurant
The	ravenous	students	devoured	a	massive	pizza	from		that	dodgy	takeaway
The	milchy	mulchers	muttled	some	moppy	mins	behind	a	multy	morridor

These examples show that words that share the same syntactical properties fill the same slots in sentences. So, the words in column 1 are all determiners. Column 2 is for adjectives, column 3 for nouns, and so on. Try replacing a word with another one from the same grammatical category – although the sentence might not make complete sense, the grammar will still be acceptable. You can try it out with nonsense words too – as I've done in sentence 3.

3.2 Phrases

In the sentences you have just read, some words appear to work with other words to create meaning: structural units known as phrases. For example, the strings of words in columns 1, 2, 3 seem to form a natural unit – as do the strings in 5, 6, 7 and 9, 10, 11. Phrases are always named after the word which is the most important – known as the *head word*. There are five types of phrase in English: noun phrases, verb phrases, adjective phrases, prepositional phrases and adverb phrases. We will look at three of them here.

3.2.1 Noun phrases

The string *the small waitress* forms a noun phrase, because the head word *waitress* is a noun. The definite article *the* points to a singular individual, and the adjective *small* works attributively (see Chapter 2) to provide more information about the noun.

We could create an even longer noun phrase, modifying the noun in all sorts of ways depending on the meanings we wanted to make and the effects we wanted to create for our text receivers: *the small, nervous, red-faced, Turkish waitress*, for example. Or, we could strip the phrase down to its bare bones and leave it as minimal as possible: *the waitress*. Text 3A is an advert for a fragrance that makes extensive use of noun phrases to create meaning:

Text 3A

CALVIN KLEIN
CK2

An urban woody fresh fragrance.
A gender-free scent for a man or a woman.
ck2 celebrates today's youth, embodies
the thrill of life and celebrates the diversity
of connections between two people. ck2
is a dual-faceted scent that balances two
opposing forces: the strike of spicy electric
freshness and the warmth of magnetic woods.
A signature fragrance for an urban, alternative,
new freshness. Fresh. Warm. Electric.

£31.00 50ml EDT

SAVE AT LEAST £4.00 ON
THE HIGH STREET PRICE

Here are some of the noun phrases used to describe the product:

An urban woody fresh fragrance

A gender-free scent

The thrill of life

The diversity of connections

Two people

Dual-faceted scent

Two opposing forces

Spicy electric freshness

Magnetic woods

Signature fragrance

Urban, alternative, new freshness

ACTIVITY 3.1
Noun phrases in discourse
Look at Text 3A and the noun phrases that follow it. Thinking about discourses and the participants involved in this text, why do you think the text producer uses such noun phrases? How are noun phrases used to position the text receiver and build an image of the ideal consumer?

3.2.2 Adjective phrases

We said that *the small, nervous, red-faced, Turkish waitress* is a noun phrase, where the head word is modified by a number of adjectives before it. In fact, we can be a little more specific than that: it is a noun phrase being modified by an adjective phrase, meaning that the entire sentence is made up of two phrases. In this example then, the adjective phrase is 'nested' inside the noun phrase. Some brackets will be useful here, to show the internal structure of the sentence:

[the [small, nervous, red-faced] waitress]

Adjective phrases do not have to be nested within other phrases, they can survive perfectly well on their own:

the waitress who was [small, nervous and red-faced]

3.2.3 Verb phrases

Verb phrases are built up around combinations of lexical verbs, auxiliary verbs and modal verbs. They are normally finite (in that they tell us about tense, aspect, person and number). The following examples of verb phrases are taken from texts from Chapters 1 and 2. The verb phrase has been underlined:

Noun phrase	Verb phrase
Captain	<u>throws</u> four men off flight
The city	<u>isn't</u> a threatening place
I	<u>am sending</u> you Zen and love from Japan
Your donation	<u>will be used</u> to make a difference

In all these examples, the verb phrase combines with the noun phrase to tell us about who or what is involved in a process or event. So, in the first example *captain* combines with the verb phrase *throws*, which combines with another noun phrase, *four men*.

3.2.3.1 Modal auxiliary verbs

In Chapter 2 we looked briefly at modal auxiliary verbs, and we now return to them to see how they work in a verb phrase. Modal auxiliary verbs combine with lexical verbs to express the degree of commitment towards an event or person, helping us to 'shade' meaning:

Modal	Meaning
can/could	possibility/ability/permission/tentativeness
may/might	possibility/permission
must	necessity/obligation
will/shall	prediction/intention
should	obligation/advice
would	intention

Compare these sentences, where the modal auxiliary verb has been changed from the original *will*:

Your donation can be used to make a difference.

Your donation might be used to make a difference.

In each instance, the modal expresses possibility about a future event. However, the meanings are rather different: *will make a difference* sounds a lot more assured than *might make a difference*, and we could argue that the text producer chose *will* for a reason: they want their text receivers (people who have donated money) to be certain that their money is going to be used for good. Chapter 4 explores the meaning of modal auxiliary verbs (and other modal forms) in more detail.

3.3 Clauses

Just as morphemes combine to form words and words combine to form phrases, phrases combine to form clauses. A clause is a group of words centred around a lexical verb phrase, containing all the extra bits (such as auxiliaries) that might be there too. Examples include (verb phrase underlined):

a few caraway seeds <u>add</u> a nutty, almost musky flavour

there <u>are</u> cycle racks opposite

they <u>should also crack down on</u> appalling grammar and spelling

A clause by itself is the main clause – but clauses often combine to form sentences, and so spotting the verb phrase(s) will tell you how many clauses there are in a sentence. Sentences that are made up of more than one clause are called multi-clause structures, built through either coordination or subordination.

KEY TERMS

Main clause: a clause which bears no relation (other than through coordination) to another clause

Multi-clause structure: a structure constructed from more than one clause

---

3.3.1 Coordination

The most familiar coordinating conjunctions are *and*, *but* and *or*. When a coordinating conjunction links two main clauses to create a compound sentence, we call this process coordination. So, examples from texts looked at so far include:

Post a message on Facebook <u>and</u> tell your friends.

Well, FIFA got its wish <u>and</u> Cristiano Ronaldo will grace the greatest show on earth next summer, <u>but</u> they'd better hit the ground running.

In each case, the main clauses that are being joined by the coordinating conjunction can stand by themselves – they are independent.

Paul Simpson (2014) suggests that the best way of conceptualising such compound structures is to use a box analogy, imagining them linked together like beads on a string:

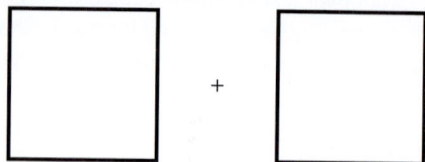

3.3.2 Subordination

Subordination involves the combining of a main clause with one or more subordinating clauses. The subordinate clauses are dependent or controlled by the main clause (hence the 'subordinate' label), meaning that the string of words introduced by the subordinator depends upon what goes before it. This means that subordinate clauses require the main clause to be present, in order to make sense and be considered grammatical. They connect items of 'unequal' status, and examples include (with the subordinator underlined):

I left early <u>because</u> I had school the next day.

I couldn't find it either, <u>although</u> I did do an extensive search.

We wondered <u>if</u> somehow this was all weather related.

So, in our boxes analogy, one would be dependent upon the other – where the main clause is the supporting box which, if taken away, will cause the subordinating clause to topple over:

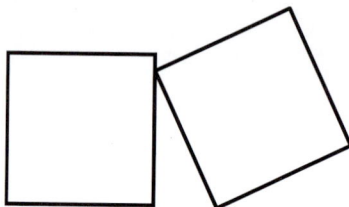

3.3.2.1 Relative clauses

Relative clauses are a type of subordinate clause, and are generally introduced by a relative pronoun (*who, which, that*) or a relative adverb (*when, where*) as in the following examples (where the relative clause is underlined):

Martin, <u>who gets up at 3 a.m. and is ready to milk 200 cows by 5 a.m.</u>

The meal, <u>which I spent all day cooking</u>, was an absolute disaster.

I can't remember <u>when I last saw such an ordinary-looking bunch of blokes on stage</u>.

In these examples, the relative clause tells us some more specific information about the noun phrase. Sometimes, the relative pronoun may be ellipted (indicated by square brackets):

Make a list of the top ten songs [that] you like.

Imagine all the people [who are] waiting outside.

> **KEY TERM**
>
> **Ellipsis:** where one or more words are omitted

Notice how in these examples, the relative clause is 'nested' inside another clause – which according to the box analogy, would be conceptualised like this:

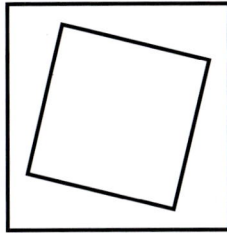

3.4 Functions

Word class labels (adjective, noun, etc.), phrases (noun phrase, etc.) and clauses (main clause, etc.) are *form* labels, describing what units of language *are*: *function* labels are related to what units *do*. This is an important way of how sentences operate as a whole unit.

Eventually, we will build up to analysing sentences to look something like this:

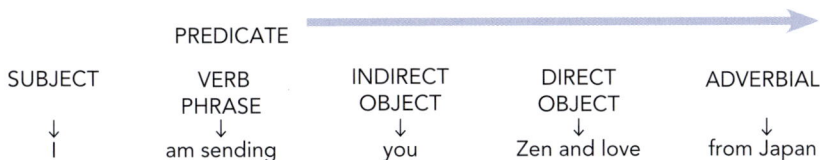

SUBJECT	PREDICATE			
	VERB PHRASE	INDIRECT OBJECT	DIRECT OBJECT	ADVERBIAL
↓	↓	↓	↓	↓
I	am sending	you	Zen and love	from Japan

- The subject is often the instigator or participant of a process expressed in the verb phrase. It is usually a noun phrase, noun or pronoun and gives us a good idea of what the theme of the sentence is about: in other words, what is being discussed. Examples include:

  Cristiano Ronaldo will grace the greatest show on earth next summer.

Text Analysis and Representation

<u>You</u>'re amazing!

<u>The British Library</u> is home to over a million books.

<u>It</u>'s raining.

An easy way to spot the subject is to ask 'who' or 'what' immediately in front of the first verb:

Who will grace the greatest show on earth next summer? *Answer = Cristiano Ronaldo*

What is home to over a million books? *Answer = The British Library*

Usually the subject is 'given' information, and the thing that follows is 'new' information, but it doesn't have to be like this:

Three hours ago <u>he</u> blundered up the trench.

And finally, the subject can change position depending on whether the sentence is making a statement (as in the above examples), or posing a question:

Did <u>Harry</u> ever find the sword of Gryffindor?

What was <u>the weather</u> like?

- The predicate is easy to spot, since it is what is left of the sentence when the subject has been removed. So, in the sentences above, the predicates are the strings of words that are not underlined. The predicate is sometimes referred to as the rheme or 'comment', in that it tells us something about the subject.

- The function of the object is to identify the entity being acted on by the action of a verb process, so they refer to a different person or thing than the subject. They can be nouns, noun phrases or pronouns, and normally come after the verb phrase. There are two kinds: direct and indirect.

  - The direct object is semantically directly 'affected' by the verb phrase.

  - The indirect object refers to the 'benefactor' or 'recipient' of the verb phrase.

SUBJECT	VP	INDIRECT OBJECT	DIRECT OBJECT
↓	↓	↓	↓
I	*am sending*	*you*	*Zen and love*

Note how the indirect object can be ellipted here: remove it, and the resulting sentence is still grammatically acceptable. Verbs that do not require an object or complement are intransitive, as in *I laughed* or *we all groaned*. Verbs that take objects are transitive, as in *they constructed the Empire State Building* or *I wrote a book*. Many verbs can be both transitive and intransitive, for example *continue*, *return* and *grow*.

- The complement is the attribute of a subject or object: it refers to the same person, thing or idea. There are two types – subject complements and object complements:

  - Subject complements often follow the copular verb (*be*, *become*, *seem*, *is*, *am*):

    Mumbai is <u>big</u>.

    She became <u>irritated</u>.

    I am normally <u>a fan</u> of the traditional apple sauce with pork.

    But can also follow other verbs:

    The future seems <u>uncertain</u>.

  - Object complements complete the meaning of the object:

    It made me <u>angry</u>.

    They made me <u>a member of the organising committee</u>.

- The adverbial can also form part of the predicate, but is optional: it can be freely added or removed without disturbing the grammatical acceptability of the clause. Its function is to identify the circumstance of the verb phrase in terms of place, time or manner. It can be an adverb phrase, prepositional phrase, noun phrase or subordinate clause:

  I am sending you Zen and love <u>from Japan</u>.

  It's a small world <u>after all</u>.

  Supper is a <u>tightwad affair of shredded</u> cabbage.

  Adverbials are fairly flexible in terms of their positioning and move about with ease in the sentence:

  <u>From Japan</u>, I am sending you Zen and love.

  <u>After all</u>, it's a small world.

  It is, <u>after all</u>, a small world.

  <u>A tightwad affair</u>, supper is shredded cabbage.

  Text producers can move adverbials to various positions in a sentence, such as the beginning, in order to draw attention to them.

> **KEY TERMS**
>
> **Subject:** often the instigator of a process expressed in the verb phrase. It is usually a noun phrase, noun or pronoun (compare with *theme*)
>
> **Theme:** a part of a sentence corresponding to what the sentence as a whole is about
>
> **Predicate:** what is left of the sentence when the subject has been removed, representing what the subject is about (compare with *rheme*)
>
> **Rheme:** a part of a sentence communicating information related to whatever is indicated by the theme
>
> **Object:** often the entity being acted on by the action of a verb process, so they refer to a different person or thing than the subject. They can be nouns, noun phrases or pronouns, and normally come after the verb phrase. There are two kinds: direct and indirect.
>
> **Intransitive verb:** a verb that does not take an object
>
> **Transitive verb:** a verb that takes one or more objects
>
> **Complement:** the attribute of a subject or object
>
> **Adverbial:** an optional part of the predicate, whose function is to identify the circumstance of the verb phrase in terms of place, time or manner. It is usually an adverb or prepositional phrase

3.5 Active and passive voice

Grammatical structures are just as important in creating meaning as any other level of language, seen as when the same event is represented in different clausal structures in what we call construal. For example:

1   The thief broke into the car.

2   The car was broken into by the thief.

3   The car was broken into.

In (1), the active voice is used, meaning that the subject, or 'agent' (the thief) is foregrounded – the thief is the theme of the sentence, and is given a privileged, attentional position in the sentence. As a result, they are absolutely to blame for the thievery! In sentence (2), the passive voice is used, drawing attention to a different grammatical subject and theme, the car. It is only at the very end of the sentence that we find out who is responsible – the thief's role is downplayed, especially when compared with (1). In sentence (3), the thief is ellipted entirely and therefore receives no attention. The perpetrator of the crime is left anonymous – even though the crime still happened. The choice of syntax (the positioning of words in a phrase, clause or sentence) is significant here, in how different meanings are created and where our attention is focused. Active and passive voice is concerned with perspective and prominence, as it allows text producers to foreground (or remove) participants or the verb process in a clause.

KEY TERMS

Active voice: where the subject is filled by an agent, who performs the action expressed by the verb

Passive voice: where the subject is filled by a patient, who receives the action expressed by the verb; the agent is omitted or placed later in the clause

Syntax: the study of how words form larger structures such as phrases, clauses and sentences

When the passive is formed, the object from the active is 'promoted' to be the new subject. The syntax of active and passive clauses is captured in Figure 3.1:

Figure 3.1: The syntax of active and passive clauses

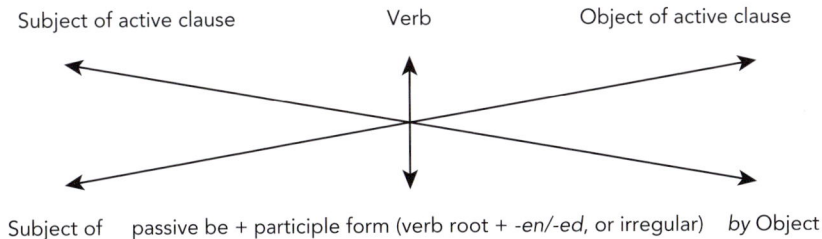

Subject of active clause   Verb   Object of active clause

Subject of   passive be + participle form (verb root + -en/-ed, or irregular)   by Object

ACTIVITY 3.2

Attention, prominence and the active/passive voice

Read Text 3B, the opening of *The War of the Worlds* by H. G. Wells. This extract describes how humans are being watched by Martians. What can you say about the choice of active/passive clauses? Who or what appears in subject or agent position, and what consequences does this have in terms of agency, attention and prominence? You could also try rewriting the text, modifying active/passive clauses so that it adds or removes prominence to certain parts.

Text 3B

No one would have believed in the last years of the nineteenth century that this world was being watched keenly and closely by intelligences greater than man's and yet as mortal as his own; that as men busied themselves about their various concerns they were scrutinised and studied, perhaps almost as narrowly as a man with a microscope might scrutinise the transient creatures that swarm and multiply in a drop of water.

Extract from *The War of the Worlds*, H.G. Wells (1898)

3.6 Sentences

We now move to the largest unit of grammar: the sentence. We will see how text producers use four sentence forms (declaratives, interrogatives, imperatives and exclamatives), which carry out different functions.

KEY TERMS

Declarative: a sentence that has a typical function to make a statement

Interrogative: a sentence that has a typical function to ask a question

Imperative: a sentence that has a typical function to issue a command

Exclamative: a sentence that has a typical function to make an expressive or emotive exclamation

3.6.1 Declaratives

The form of declarative sentences is that the subject precedes the predicate. The normal function of declarative sentences is to make a statement about something, and they are by far the most common type in English. Examples are:

The thief broke into the car.

The city isn't a threatening place.

3.6.2 Interrogatives

The form of interrogatives is that one part of the predicate precedes the subject, usually the first verb:

operator (finite auxiliary) ⟶ predicate ⟶ subject

The most typical function of an interrogative is to ask a question. Declaratives can be formed into interrogatives, as in:

Who broke into the car?

Is the city a threatening place?

3.6.3 Imperatives

Imperatives need not have an overt subject, and usually start with a verb:

Trim the fat in just days!

Slice the cabbage across the grain into thin shreds.

Even though there is no subject in these sentences, the intended subject in each case is clearly the text receiver, or the second person you – 'you can trim the fat in just days'; 'you must slice the cabbage across the grain into thin shreds'.

The function of an imperative is therefore to issue orders or commands.

The bare imperative form actually appears relatively rarely, and can sound rude outside very formal or authoritative contexts. An imperative function is often 'softened' by a politeness marker (such as *please*), or is replaced by a declarative or interrogative – a good example of where distinguishing between structure and function is important.

Imperative *form* ⟶ **Transformation to imperative *function***

Pass me the ketchup.   *Can you pass me the ketchup?* (interrogative form)

I wonder if you'd mind passing me the ketchup. (declarative form)

Ketchup on chips is heaven. (declarative form)

Go and brush your hair.   *Have you brushed your hair yet?* (interrogative form)

I wish you would brush your hair. (declarative form)

Your hair needs brushing. (declarative form)

Interpretation of these forms therefore relies heavily on context and intended meanings, which is related to pragmatics (discussed in Chapter 4). It would be very odd (and irritating) if somebody were to reply with 'yes' to 'can you pass me the ketchup?', instead of actually doing it.

3.6.4 Exclamatives

The form of exclamatives is very distinctive:

what or how phrase ——→ subject ——→ predicate

For example:

What a load of old rubbish!

What a nightmare performance!

The function of exclamatives is fairly restricted – they are (not surprisingly) used to make an expressive or emotive exclamation about something.

3.6.5 Clause patterns in classroom discourse

Text 3C is a transcript from a Year 7 (age 11–12) English lesson, recorded in a UK secondary school in June 2016. The teacher (T) and students (S) are discussing a poem.

Text 3C

S1:   you know when it says 'your arm approaches and it closes' (.) does that mean your hand?

T: it could do (.) we've got that word **it** (.) that could be referring to your hand or what else?

S1:   your hand (.) or it could be the jellyfish

T: yep (.) so it might refer to both (.) or just one of them (1) you decide (.) think about what was in **your** own head when **you** read it

S2:   could it be both at the same time?

T: if you like (.) what's funny about that word 'it' in this poem? hands up

S3:   we don't know what it is describing (.) it might be your hand or the jellyfish

T: absolutely (.) what kind of word is it?

S1:   a pronoun? I don't know

T: **good**! what a star! yep (.) ok (.) just half a minute more guys (.) think about these bits in red

Even in such a short space of time, the participants use a range of different sentence forms and functions. Interrogatives are a common feature of classroom discourse, used by both teachers and students. The teacher uses the function to request information and as a way of assessing student knowledge ('what kind of word is it?'; 'what's funny about that word "it" in this poem?'). Here, the teacher is in the role of the powerful participant (Fairclough, 2001) – using interrogatives to check student progress and to steer the direction of the lesson in various ways. Students use the interrogative function in slightly different ways – to check and monitor *their own* progress and understanding, but also to suggest they are uncertain about expressing themselves in response to the teacher's interrogatives ('does that mean your hand?'; 'could it be both at the same time?'; 'a pronoun?').

KEY TERM

Powerful participant: the participant that holds the most power in a given discourse and context

The declarative function is again used by the teacher to propel the lesson forward and provide information ('just half a minute more guys'; 'we've got that word "it"'). Students use the declarative to provide responses to interrogatives ('your hand (.) or it could be the jellyfish'; 'we don't know what it's describing'; 'I don't know').

Imperatives play an important functional role for the teacher, providing a way of issuing commands and directives for what they want the students to do ('hands up'; 'think about these bits in red').

The only exclamative is used to function as praise: 'what a star!'

RESEARCH QUESTION
Grammar and authority

Text 3D is a Road Safety Road Show Voucher issued by the City of London Police. This was given to me by a police officer after I (mistakenly) cycled through a red light. As well as providing an opportunity for me to reflect on my own cycling habits, it provides a fascinating example of what I will call 'authoritative grammar'. There are a number of grammatical features that create a sense of power and authority, which, combined with the wider discourse of law enforcement, offer a remarkably intimidating text. Use the following bullet points as a guide for analysis:

- How are noun, verb and adjective phrases built up and what kind of specificity do they offer about things, places and events? Why might a text like this offer such specificity?

- How are modal auxiliary verbs used in determining the choices, obligations and permissions the text receiver has?

- How are clauses built up through coordination and subordination? How are the coordinate clauses linked together? What kinds of patterns exist between main clauses and subordinate/relative clauses?

- Are active or passive constructions used? What is the significance of this? Who or what is given prominence in sentences?

- The various sentence functions and how these provide information and issue commands.

- The kind of relationship built between text producer and text receiver, such as through the pronoun system.

- How might the register, genre, participants and discourse affect the grammatical choices of this text?

- Once you have worked through these, find another text that imposes authority and limitations on its text receiver(s). What connections can you see between the two? Do they draw on similar grammatical choices? Can you come to some kind of conclusions about the grammar of authority?

Text 3D

CITY of LONDON POLICE

Road Safety Road Show Voucher

You have been issued with a fixed penalty ticket for committing a road traffic offence under the Road Traffic Act 1988 whilst riding a pedal cycle.

You can pay the £30 fixed penalty or have your ticket replaced with an educational warning by using this voucher to attend a Road Safety road show. You can 'drop in' at any time between 08:00 am and 10:00 am. The session will last a **minimum of 40 minutes** and will take place at Dowgate fire station, Upper Thames Street, London EC4R 3UE. (see map overleaf) on Friday 22nd February 2013. Secure cycle parking is available at the venue.

There will be no entry after 10:00 am.

If you do not wish to attend the road show, then please follow the instructions on payment given with your ticket.

Terms and Conditions:

This voucher can only be used at the Road Safety road show detailed above.
No other voucher will be accepted.
This voucher is not transferable.
The option of attending a Road Safety road show and thus avoiding a fixed penalty does not apply if you have already attended a road show in the last two years.
Please bring your issued ticket, identification with your name and address and this voucher with you to the road show in order to have your ticket replaced with a warning.

Officer please complete all parts below when issuing ticket

Was the rider....	YES	NO
..on a TfL HIRE CYCLE		X
..distracted (i.e. using ear phones)		X

Wider reading

Read about the grammar of English and stylistics in more detail, by exploring the following books:

Aarts, B. (2011) *Oxford Modern English Grammar*. Oxford: Oxford University Press.

Huddleston, R. and Pullum, G.K. (2005) *A Student's Introduction to English Grammar*. Cambridge: Cambridge University Press.

Simpson, P. (2014) *Stylistics: A Resource Book for Students* (Second edition). London: Routledge.

Tallerman, M. (2014) *Understanding Syntax* (Fourth edition). London: Routledge.

Quirk, R., Greenbaum, S., Leech, G. and Svartvik, J. (1985) *A Comprehensive Grammar of the English Language*. London: Longman.

Chapter 4
Creating meaning

In this chapter you will:

- Explore further ways that meanings are made in language

- Consider how context affects meaning

- Apply this knowledge to text analysis

Text Analysis and Representation

The previous chapters have provided an introduction to the structural features of English. Whilst we have considered textual meaning throughout, we now turn our attention to a range of concepts in linguistics that are of further use in considering how meanings are made and negotiated.

4.1 Negotiating meaning: semantics and pragmatics

Semantics and pragmatics are the study of meaning in language – how and why words, phrases, clauses and sentences mean what they do. In participating in discourse, we *negotiate* meaning: we choose language that is most appropriate for the context that we find ourselves in.

KEY TERMS

Semantics: the branch of linguistics concerned with the study of meaning. This includes the meaning of words and their combinations into larger structures (phrases, clauses and sentences)

Pragmatics: the branch of linguistics concerned with language in use – including how context shapes meaning, choices and interpretations

Language is a tool that we use to understand and explain the world. But this is never straightforward, and language is far from perfect. Objects in the world have many names: the key in my pocket is not only a 'key', it is a 'metal object', a 'tool', and a 'thing'. It also has a more specific meaning: it is a 'front door key' *to* 'a London flat', and it has a unique pattern of scratches and colours. Furthermore, whilst there is only one of these unique keys to open a unique lock, there are tens of thousands of 'front door keys to London flats' in the world. Similarly, the cat outside my window is not only a 'cat', but is a 'tabby', a 'mammal', an 'animate being', and so on. But to engage in successful and practical communication, most contexts do not require us to refer to such specific objects. The word 'key', in most contexts will be sufficient to make an intended meaning. In participating in discourse, we negotiate meaning: we choose language that is most appropriate for the context that we find ourselves in.

To negotiate meaning, participants require a good understanding of semantics and pragmatics. Essentially, the semantic meaning of a word is its literal meaning: a 'key' denotes a physical item in the world that has a particular shape, material and function. Indeed, my dictionary tells me that it is a 'small piece of shaped metal with incisions cut to fit the wards of a particular lock'. The majority of people participating in discourse would agree and understand this. But it also has other meanings: it's a button on a keyboard, which I am pressing now, and it's a lever on a musical instrument. There are others too (my dictionary lists a total of 13). Lots of words carry multiple meanings like this. How then, are we ever to know which meaning people are referring to? The answer of course, lies in context. Consider the following exchange:

A: ready?

B: yep (.) have you got the key?

A: in my bag

You can probably work out the context here: two people leaving a building. Because of our understanding of this familiar context, we understand that the word 'key' refers to a small metal object used for locking and unlocking doors, rather than its other meanings. Language always operates in a context, and context is the crucial factor in negotiating meaning. The study of how context affects meaning is known as pragmatics. Compare these examples of 'key':

Economic freedom is the key to all freedom.

Slow, prolonged heat is the key to good ribs.

Clearly there is no physical key here: it is being used in an abstract, metaphorical sense. We know this because of the other words it is being used with: again, context is a fundamental part of the meaning-making process. The connotations of 'key' are the further associations or 'secondary meaning'. Colours are a good way of demonstrating the difference between connotation and denotation: the word 'red' denotes the physical properties of the particular point in the colour spectrum, but in many cultures connotes things such as anger, love and danger.

KEY TERMS

Denotation: the literal or primary meaning of a word

Connotation: the overtones associated with a word or phrase

4.2 Knowledge

Language provides different meanings for different people, and the same text may even mean something different to the same person, but in a different context. Elizabeth Bates (1979) provides a metaphor of an iceberg for the total sense of a word to its user: the visible tip represents the 'public aspect' of meaning, resting on the submerged base of 'private meaning'. Whereas 'public meaning' refers to usages or meanings found in dictionaries, 'private meaning' is the connotations and schemas that a word holds for a particular individual. A schema is a bundle of information built up from our experience in the world. An individual's private schema and meaning may or may not agree with the public version, and words involve a mix of both public and private elements: the base as well as the tip of the semantic iceberg. Louise Rosenblatt suggests her own metaphor of access to individual meaning: a 'linguistic-experiential reservoir' (Rosenblatt 2005), which is the residue of an individual's past experiences, accumulated over time. Participants will then draw on their own linguistic-experiential 'reservoirs', 'icebergs' and schemas when engaging in discourse. But crucially, participants need only activate certain schemas at certain times: if I need to order a drink in a pub, I use my schematic knowledge of pubs, but in this context my schematic knowledge of say, repairing bicycles, is unlikely to be required and remains in the background. So, the discourse context acts as a kind of 'filter' to control and limit the kind of knowledge that participants need to access in order to deal with different situations.

KEY TERM

Schema: a bundle of knowledge about a concept, person or event

---

ACTIVITY 4.1

Knowledge and schemas in texts

Look back at Text 1G from Chapter 1 (*Men's Health* magazine cover). What kind of schematic knowledge is the text producer assuming of their audience, and prompting them to activate? How does this position the audience? How might a *lack* of schematic knowledge be used to exclude or limit certain audiences?

4.3 Networks of words

Words don't exist in isolation – they exist alongside other words to create networks and patterns of meaning. There are various ways of exploring this, which we will do in the following sections.

4.3.1 Semantic fields

One way of exploring word networks and patterns is through the notion of *semantic fields*, which are groups of words based around a topic or theme. For example, *keyboard*, *mouse* and *megabyte* are all members of the semantic field of 'computers'. Text producers will use different semantic fields depending on the purpose, register or genre of a text – for example, a magazine article about computers is likely to use words from the semantic field of computers, and so on. This book draws on the semantic field of 'linguistics', and the glossary of metalanguage at the end of this book is a good example of a semantic field.

4.3.2 Collocation

Some words have common associations with other words, and are often used habitually with one another: known as collocates. For example, *blonde* collocates with *hair*, and *strong* collocates with *tea*. Collocations create meaning through their association, and there are around six main structures:

- adjective + noun (e.g. *clear water*)

- noun + noun (e.g. *tap water*)

- verb + noun (e.g. *to boil water*)

- adverb + adjective (e.g. *bitterly cold*)

- verb + preposition (e.g. *apply to*)

- verb + adverb (e.g. *walk briskly*)

> **KEY TERM**
>
> **Collocates:** words that typically appear together

Collocation analysis is a common part of corpus linguistics, the analysis of enormous data sets (or 'corpora') using computer software. In an analysis of the language of Tony Blair's 'New Labour' party (the UK government between 1997 and 2010) Norman Fairclough (2000) found that 'work' collocated with 'into', 'back to' and 'desire to' more than with 'out of', suggesting the kinds of messages and policies that the government wanted to promote. Even seemingly innocuous or neutral words (such as the verb 'create') can be part of collocations that display interesting patterns. For example, Text 4A is a screenshot of 'create' as it exists in a corpus search:

Text 4A

t on his laurels. He **pushed** himself to	create	more elaborate masterpieces. In
ir own adventures. The museum **was** created		to ensure the opportunity for safe explorati
<p> She **decided** the solution was to	create	a brand of her own. </p><p> "I decided tl
for a new dawn. It will not **be** easy to	create	order in that ruined country, the skeptics tr
nered home the advantage. We **were creating**		space and keeping Ireland on the back foot
at of not **knowing** all the details that	creates	anxiety. But progress is progress." <p
health officials **say** disconnections will	create	hygiene and health problems. Mi
very penny he **earned** . He wanted to	create	an eco village. He never cared about himse
oductive for generations to **come** and	creating	a food system that supports its community
rld's resources. This **is** not just unfair,	creating	huge differences in standards of living, it al
ble Scottish Orangemen might **play** in	creating	a better future. Arguably, the annual visita
ly's GDP. The Camorra **has** created		a clever circle of illegal business, Mafia wat
this kind of population growth. It **has** created		a lot of strain," said planning director Chris
bu allow women to take a pill, you **are creating**		a dependency and they will never take resp
ne economy, **demoralizes** voters and	creates	civic unrest. Former President Je
and Gordon Ramsay **moved** in -but it	created	a stir. Vongerichten wants to she
ggle to cope with the influx of patients	created	by **centralising** services. David Sedgwick
ken a different path and I **think** we've	created	greater value. I think it's fair to say we are
e might do in an evening of new work,	created	to **be** seen all at once. One thing she estab
agencies agree that the PDA **hopes** to	create	tension in advance of the elections in Nove
he **aggravated** damages. The judges	created	a stir when they concluded that the way ar
h was first **mooted** last month, would	create	a Pounds 1.3 billion company in the kitcher
ing in 2010 and **have** the potential to	create	the first truly global broadband wireless ne
experts said the move **was** unlikely to	create	significant problems for Santander's bid bu
ty with the sea that **makes** us long to	create	a nautical atmosphere in our gardens, whe
mocrats. He **said** the new boundaries	created	just what was intended: more "swing" distr
, Welch **said** , because their sacrifices	created	the life and faith that Irish Americans enjoy
erstanding of the risks of Avandia **had**	created	excessive concern, depressing sales of the

Collocates of 'create' from the Cambridge English Corpus

It's interesting to note here that 'create' isn't as innocent or neutral as we thought. The patterns in the corpus show that it can have negative connotations ('created excessive concern'; 'create tension'; 'creates anxiety'). The semantics of words are only revealed when we consider the various contexts in which they can appear.

4.3.3 Categories and prototypes

Words and their meanings do not fall neatly into groups or categories. For example, consider the category of 'birds'. 'Blackbirds', 'robins' and 'doves' would be good, prototypical or 'central' examples of words that fall into this category, but 'penguins' and 'ostriches' would not – they are less good, or 'peripheral' members of the category. This distribution of category membership can be displayed in a radial structure, as shown in Figure 4.1.

Figure 4.1: Prototypes: 'good' birds and 'less good' birds

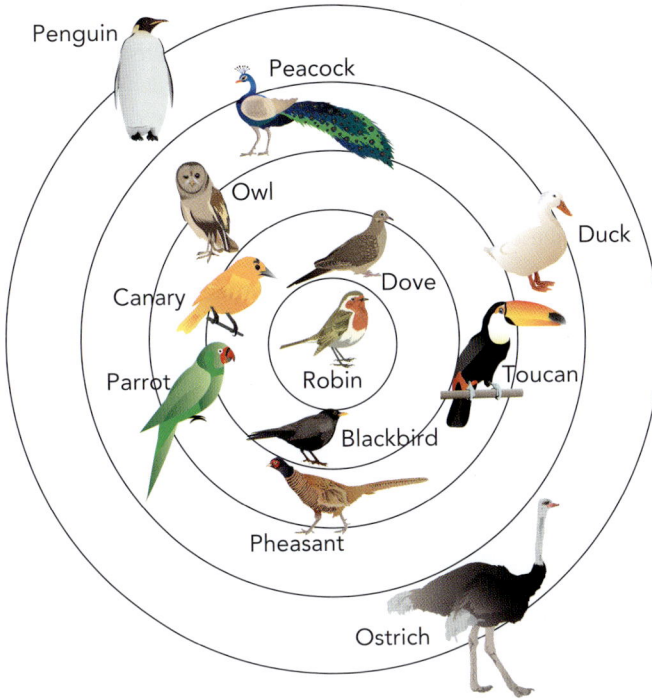

This way of categorising language is known as 'prototype theory', first proposed by Eleanor Rosch (1975). Later work by George Lakoff (1987) suggested that our knowledge of the world is organised by 'idealised cognitive models' (ICM), where words often do not fully capture the whole complexity of reality. A famous example is the question 'is the Pope a bachelor?'. In most people's ICM of 'bachelor', this suggests an unmarried, single, (often young) male, who is a good candidate for marriage. Our ICM of 'pope', a man who holds a commitment to the Catholic church, which forbids ordained priests to marry, means that the pope is clearly not a 'good example' of a bachelor! We hold ICMs for all words, many of which trigger various connotations and metaphorical associations. At the centre of ICMs are prototypes, and the features that most strongly define them – for example, a 'blackbird' is a prototypical example of a 'bird' – it has two wings, has a beak, is small, and can fly. 'Penguins', 'ostriches' and other 'less birdy' birds are far from prototypical, but remain 'birds' nonetheless.

4
4.4 Metaphor

Many people usually think of metaphor as being confined to the study of literary texts, but as we shall see, it infiltrates everyday discourse and is a crucial way of understanding how language is used to represent the world. In their work on metaphor, George Lakoff and Mark Johnson (1980) demonstrated that text producers use metaphor to make sense of abstract concepts by understanding them in terms of more physical ones. Some common metaphors (small capitals are used to show these) include:

LIFE IS A JOURNEY	*I'm at the middle-age crossroads.*
	We're moving forward with the plans.
TIME IS MONEY	*I can't afford to spend any more time on this.*
	I've invested a lot of time in that.
UP IS GOOD /	*Things are looking up.*
DOWN IS BAD	*He does high-quality work.*
	He's going through a period of depression.
	This country is sinking into austerity.
POLITICS IS A BATTLE	*I have fought long and hard to win this election.*
	This party is making victims out of the most disadvantaged.

KEY TERM

Metaphor: a structure that presents one thing in terms of another

---

Metaphor is a way of seeing one 'domain' of knowledge in terms of another: an 'abstract' target domain mapped on to a 'concrete' source domain. Concrete domains are those things that we are likely to encounter in the physical world. So, in the metaphor LIFE IS A JOURNEY, we understand the abstract domain of 'life' in terms of a common physical, embodied experience of a 'journey' and blend knowledge from the two domains to form new meaning.

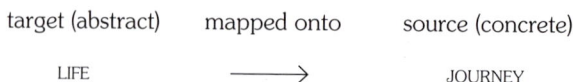

target (abstract)   mapped onto   source (concrete)

LIFE   ⟶   JOURNEY

Metaphors provide a structure or template for understanding how the text producer wants us to conceptualise certain things. Text 4B is an extract from a 2016 speech given by Justine Greening, who at the time, was the newly appointed Secretary of

State for Education in Britain. Here, she uses the metaphors of LIFE IS A JOURNEY and EDUCATION IS A BODY PART to talk about education.

Text 4B

> Our Prime Minister has talked about making sure that Britain is a country
> where everyone can be successful no matter where they start, and
> education is clearly at the heart of how we are going to ensure that
> happens. I do not believe that anybody's starting point in life should
> define where they finish. I did not accept that for myself and I do not think
> we should accept it for anyone else. Education is at the heart of how we
> tackle that issue of improving social mobility.
>
> Extract from a speech by Justine Greening (2016)

LIFE IS A JOURNEY	everyone can be successful no matter where they start
	I do not believe that anybody's starting point in life should define where they finish
EDUCATION IS A BODY PART	education is clearly at the heart of how we are going to ensure that happens
	education is at the heart of how we tackle that issue

In using these two metaphors, the text producer is clear in her ideologies, values and world-views. The LIFE IS A JOURNEY metaphor implies that people make choices in how they move from A to B, and that access to education is one part of that 'journey'. The EDUCATION IS A BODY PART metaphor draws on our understanding of the heart as the central or innermost part of something; a vital part of all life. Both these metaphors project education as a fundamental aspect of society, but one that is dynamic and governed by individuals' choices.

Zoltan Kövecses (2002) gives a list of common source and target domains:

Common source domains

The human body; health and illness; animals; plants; building and constructions; machines and tools; games and sport; business transactions; cooking and food; heat and cold; light and darkness; forces; movement; direction

Common target domains

Emotion; desire; morality; thought; society; politics; the economy; human relationships; communication; time; life and death; religion; events; actions

You can try out the process of creating your own metaphors by taking a target domain at random and mapping it onto different source domains. For example, we could create the mapping of POLITICS IS A MACHINE and then list metaphors such as 'the government cogs have grinded to a halt', 'the new political leader needs a software update' or 'the well-oiled voting system'. Which mappings are more productive than others, and why might this be?

4.4.1 Metaphor and representation

Research by the linguist Elena Semino demonstrates how illness and recovery, in relation to cancer in particular, is represented through metaphor – for example, as a battle ('losing the battle against cancer'; 'determined to fight the disease') and a journey ('the long hard road of cancer treatment'). Her research suggested these kinds of metaphors, that often lead to feelings of failure and guilt among terminally ill patients, can have damaging effects on people's self-esteem and attitudes towards their condition. In a 2014 interview with *The Independent*, Semino suggests:

> we would say that the battle metaphor is not one that a healthcare professional should ever introduce first […] if a patient uses it, and it seems to be working well for the patient then there's no reason to challenge it. If a patient says: 'I feel a failure because I'm not winning the battle,' then I think the metaphor should be challenged. [The doctor should say]: 'It's not a battle – it's not you who is losing, we just don't have the medication to help you'.

ACTIVITY 4.2
Metaphors in political discourse

Text 4C is the opening text from the Conservative Party's 2015 manifesto. Read the text through, and then identify the different types of metaphor the text producer uses. What source and target domains are used, and why might this be? How are different groups (political parties, the public; the country as a whole) represented?

Text 4C

Over the last five years, we have put our country back on the right track. Five years ago, Britain was on the brink. As the outgoing Labour Treasury Minister put it with brutal candour, 'there is no money'. Since then, we have turned things around.

Britain is now one of the fastest growing major economies in the world. We are getting our national finances back under control. We have halved our deficit as a share of our economy. More people are in work than ever before. Britain is back on its feet, strong and growing stronger every day.

Extract from the Conservative Party's 2015 manifesto

4.5 Modality

In Chapters 2 and 3 we looked at some of the grammatical features of modal verbs, and we now return to look at some of their semantic properties, and how they fit into the system of modality more generally. Remember that modal auxiliary verbs combine with lexical verbs to express the degree of commitment towards an event or person, helping us to 'shade' meaning. Modal verbs, however, are just one part of modality: a bigger system related to a speaker's attitude to, confidence in, perception about something in the world. Ilse Depraetere and Susan Reed's (2006) definition of modality is rather lengthy, but captures it nicely:

> Modal meaning crucially involves the notions of necessity and possibility [and] a speaker's judgement that a proposition is possibly or necessarily true or that the actualization of a situation is necessary or possible.

As well as modal auxiliary verbs, modality includes lexical verbs such as *believe*, *wish* and *want*, and adjectives and adverbs such as *possible*, *possibly* and *perhaps*. When a modal form is used, it often expresses something about future events, contrasting present time with the future. For example, *a new government will get our economy moving* projects a future world where a new government have won an election, is in power, and have improved the economy.

4.5.1 Modal force

Modality is sometimes categorised into three types: deontic modality, epistemic modality and boulomaic modality.

- Deontic modality is concerned with obligation and permission:

  You <u>will</u> go to the ball

  You <u>must</u> arrive before 10 a.m.

- Epistemic modality is concerned with possibility:

  you <u>can</u> pay the £30 fixed penalty or have your ticket replaced with an educational warning

  that <u>could</u> be referring to your hand or what else?

- Boulomaic modality is concerned with wishes and desires:

  I already <u>want</u> to come back

  I <u>wish</u> you would brush your hair

KEY TERMS

Deontic modality: expressions that highlight a sense of obligation or necessity

Epistemic modality: expressions that highlight degrees of belief, certainty or perception

Boulomaic modality: expressions that highlight aspects of desire

---

A semantic property of the deontic and epistemic modal forms is that they can be classified in terms of their 'strength' or 'force'. A nice way of looking at this is by placing them on a continuum that goes from weak to strong (adapted from Giovanelli, 2014) and these are shown in Figure 4.2:

Figure 4.2 Semantic properties of deontic and epistemic modal forms

Deontic modals:

MAY	OUGHT TO	MUST
permission	*obligation*	*necessity*

Epistemic modals:

MIGHT	WILL	MUST
possible	*most possible*	*only possibility*

The use of modality is particularly interesting in texts that hold a certain amount of power over their text receivers. Consider Text 4D, an extract from a British Airways boarding pass:

Text 4D

BAG DROP

Opens
05:00

Checked baggage to: Bag Drop
Closes: 45 minutes before departure
Take your boarding pass to a Bag Drop
desk in zones B, C, D, F, or G

SECURITY

Clear Security By
06:30

If you do not clear security by the
time indicated above you will not be
accepted for your flight

BOARDING

Gate closes
06:45

If you arrive late at the gate, your bags
might be taken off the plane and you
may not be allowed to board.

Hand baggage only

Customers with hand baggage only should go to a Passport and Visa check desk located at
desks B16 or H1 before going to Security.

Hand baggage allowance
Please see ba.com

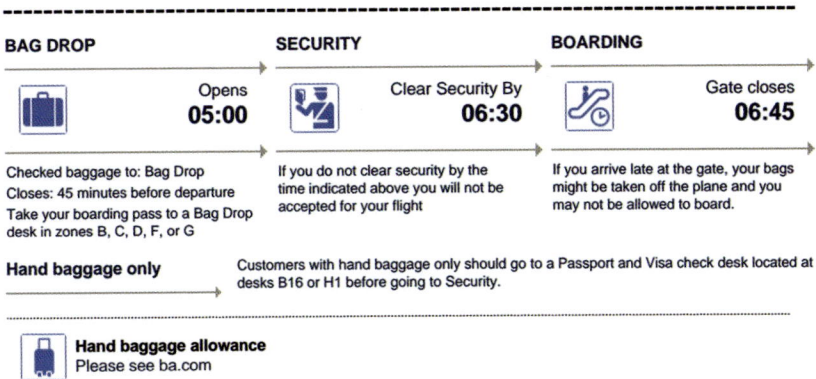

As always, the context and discourse surrounding the text is important, and a useful 'way in' to analysing the text. As an institutional text producer, British Airways hold a significant amount of power over the text receiver. Air travel incorporates a large number of rules and restrictions, and the text producer is empowered to impose these on the text receiver, expressed through a range of linguistic choices. There is extensive use of the second-person singular pronoun 'you' to address the text receiver directly. The text producer is also addressed through imperative structures (e.g. 'clear security by 06:30'; 'take your boarding pass to a bag drop desk') and conditional clauses ('if you do not clear security by the time indicated above'; 'if you arrive late at the gate'), to position the text receiver as somebody with responsibility to behave according to a very specific set of rules and conditions. Forceful deontic modals ('you will not be accepted') are used to provide a clear and direct message about the importance of arriving at the airport and clearing security on time. Weaker epistemic modals ('your bags might be taken off the plane') suggest the possibility of something slightly less drastic happening, but the weaker epistemic ('you may not be allowed to board') is used to project the airline's authority and power of the text producer. Modal force then, is a useful feature of language to consider when looking at texts that assert power over text receivers.

4.5.2 Modal shading

When texts draw upon a particular type or force of modality, it can create patterns and an overall 'feeling'. There are three types of modal shading: positive, negative and neutral. In a text with positive shading, the general 'feel' of the language will be strong and assertive. Deontic and boulomaic modal words are likely to be used. Texts that use negative shading are likely to use epistemic modal words to suggest feelings of uncertainty and anxiety. Finally, texts that use neutral shading have a complete absence of modal forms, meaning that feelings and opinions are withheld and the text has an overall 'objective' feel.

4.6 Building and representing the world

Texts present a version of the world that is filtered through a text producer's linguistic choices. In doing so, text producers can choose to draw attention or highlight certain things that they feel are important – which may or may not align with a text receiver's attitude towards the world. In this section, we look at three important concepts from cognitive linguistics, a branch of study that investigates language and mind.

4.6.1 Attention and prominence: foregrounding

Foregrounding is a popular term used in text analysis, offering a way of thinking about certain linguistic choices that text producers make and the stylistic effect of these. In discussing foregrounding, we are considering the conscious nature of crafting language, and what text producers have chosen to bring to our attention or made prominent. The things that are foregrounded in a text stand out against the background, and typically receive more attention from the text receiver, because they establish and break expected patterns. Foregrounding 'works' because we all have typical expectations of how language is used, which are built up from our experiences in the world. When those usual patterns or expectations are emphasised or broken, they stand out and create a sense of interest and surprise.

> **KEY TERM**
>
> **Foregrounding:** drawing attention to a key aspect in a text

Foregrounding can occur in a number of ways at different language levels. Here are some examples:

- **Phonology**: raised volume in spoken language; stress on certain syllables or words; rhyme; alliteration.

- **Morphology**: use of unusual inflections such as infixes; creative use of inflectional or derivational morphology (e.g. 'awesomer').

- **Lexis**: use of unusual or low-frequency lexis (words that are not commonly used); use of a particular register; repetition of words.

- **Grammar**: use of unusual structures and syntax, for example placing adverbial or subordinate clauses at the beginning of a sentence; the passive voice.

- **Semantics**: use of semantic fields to create a sense of lexical 'intensity' and to highlight a particular thing; unusual or unexpected collocations.

- **Graphology and text design**: the use of capital letters to stand out against other lower case letters; certain colour choices (e.g. red text against a white background); larger font sizes; dynamic images or text against a static background; image choices and image placement.

Things can be foregrounded through two main methods: *parallelism* or *deviation*. Parallelism involves the creation of patterns, often through repetition. Deviation involves breaking patterns away from the expected and established norms, either from outside the text or the patterns that have been established within the text itself.

Look again at Text 3D, where there are a number of features foregrounded:

- Parallelism of negation, to limit the text receivers options and choices in what they can do next: *There will be <u>no</u> entry after 10a.m.; this voucher is <u>not</u> transferable*

- Parallelism of the second-person pronoun + modal verb such as *you can* and *you will* to suggest certainty and authority, but also to give the text receiver a sense of choice.

- Sentence patterns: foregrounding is achieved through parallelism of declarative clauses/sentences, to provide information (e.g. *The session will last a minimum of 40 minutes*). This pattern is broken with the occasional use of imperatives (e.g. *please bring your issued ticket…*) creating foregrounding through deviation.

- Use of bold formatting to foreground key messages and ideas: *CITY OF LONDON POLICE; Terms and Conditions*

4.6.2 Pointing and showing: deixis

Imagine two people next to each other in the same room. One of them says to the other 'come here and look at this'. Because they share the same immediate context, each of the speakers will understand what is meant by 'here' and 'this'. This is called deixis: words that are context-bound and whose meaning depends on who is using them, and where and when they are being used. There are three main types, or deictic categories:

- **Perceptual deixis**: names and personal pronouns

- **Spatial deixis**: adverbs of place (such as *here* and *there*); demonstratives showing location (such as *this* and *that*); orientational adjectives and adverbs (such as *left*, *right* and *forward*); deictic verbs of motion (such as *come* and *go*)

- **Temporal deixis**: adverbs of time (such as *next week* and *today*); prepositional phrases (such as *in ten minutes* and *four hours ago*)

4 Text Analysis and Representation

The word 'deixis' is from a Greek verb, meaning 'pointing' or 'showing', indicating what person, object, location or event in time and space a deictic word is referring to. So, the sentence 'I am here now' points to a specific set of contextual parameters: in my kitchen, in south London, on the 28 March 2017 at 11.46 a.m. If I was to say the same sentence again tomorrow, when I will be on a train to Sheffield, it will mean a very different thing. Deictic words anchor objects and events in a particular point in time and space, and the point of 'origin' is known as the deictic centre. In our sentence above, 'come here and look at this', both speakers share the same deictic centre. Deictic words can be 'distal', pointing to things that are located far away in time and space from the deictic centre, or they can be 'proximal', where they point to things that are close by. The axes in Figure 4.3 show the different dimensions of deictic terms:

Figure 4.3: Deixis

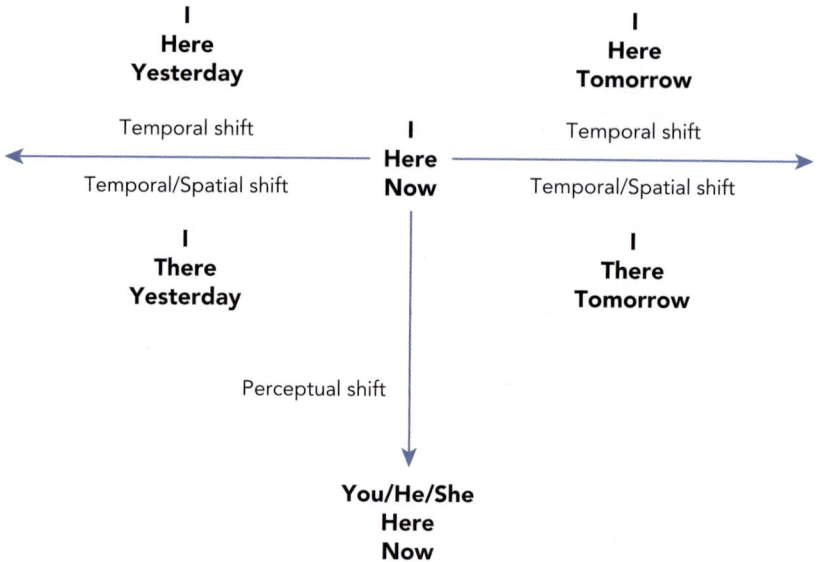

Text 4E is a transcript from a cinema, a pre-recorded message played to customers before a film starts, and demonstrates how deictic words are an integral part of the meaning-making process.

Text 4E

OK now we're ready for the main event. So, switch off your mobile phone screen, finish your conversation – that's right you two in the middle row, I can see you. You can check your messages later. Put that away! We are about to begin.

Here, deictic terms are used to address the text receiver directly through the use of proximal person deixis, the first person 'I' and the second person 'you'. The effect of this is that the deictic centre is established and maintained throughout the whole text – although this text is clearly a pre-recorded message produced without any specific individual in mind, anybody listening to the text will 'feel' as if the text is talking directly to them. They are *positioned* or framed as an individual – in what Fairclough (2001) calls 'synthetic personalisation'. The plural first person *we* also locates the text producer in the same deictic space as the text receiver. Temporal deixis ('now'; 'about to begin') and proximal spatial deixis ('put that away'; 'in the middle row') also focus the text producer's attention on the deictic centre. Finally, there is use of distal temporal deixis ('later') to project a future time frame in which the text receiver will be able to look at their mobile phone once more.

4.6.3 Analysing what isn't: negation

A particularly fascinating aspect of language is the capacity it affords participants to conceptualise the world not only in terms of what *does* happen, but also in terms of what does *not*. Negation is the process by which this happens, creating implied, rather than explicit, meanings in a text. Read this sentence and think very carefully about what happens in your mind as you do so:

Don't think of an elephant.

KEY TERM

Negation: an act of denial, a negative statement, a refusal or contradiction, marked through linguistic forms such as *no, not* and *never*

Chances are you thought of an elephant – even though the sentence is negated with 'don't'. So, in order to reject the thought of an elephant, we must first conceptualise it, before removing it. Texts don't just talk about what *is* there, they talk about what isn't there, creating hypothetical versions of reality which may be powerfully persuasive. Negation is an act of denial, a negative statement, a refusal or a contradiction, marked through linguistic forms such as *no, not, never, won't*, and so on. When we process negation, it alerts us to possible alternative scenarios: the mention of something that does *not* exist can trigger in our minds a situation where it *does* exist – as proven earlier, when I asked you not to think of an elephant. Robert Hodge and Gunther Kress (1994) put it like this:

A negative is a convenient way of expressing forbidden meanings, evading a censor by the vehemence of the denial. It is also a way of planting ideas without any responsibility for them... Negatives can create a universe of alternative meanings which the speaker formally renounces but which exists as a result of his renunciation.

This means that negation can create ideological effects, if the text producer is attempting to influence the text receiver towards imagining the 'positive' version:

> We'll also do things that <u>won't</u> cost the government much but will make a big difference.

> Over 3.5 million employees who want to work more hours but <u>can't</u>.

> There will be <u>no</u> entry after 10.00 a.m.

> Scientists warn there may be <u>no</u> ice at the North Pole this summer.

Or, negation can be used to 'sensationalise' events, such as in news reporting, where the desire for 'news as entertainment' is strong – as in this opening paragraph from a 2008 story published in *The Guardian*:

> <u>No</u> murders took place at the care home at the centre of a child abuse investigation, the new police chief leading the inquiry said today.

So, even when the story is reporting on the absence of murders, the negation still manages to trigger the idea in the text receiver's mind.

ACTIVITY 4.3
Negation in advertising

Text 4F is an advert to recruit people to join the British Army. How does the text use negation to try and persuade its audience to do this? What is conceptualised through the negation? What do you think the dominant-hegemonic reading is here, and what kind of discourses is the text producer drawing on?

Text 4F

DON'T JOIN THE ARMY.
DON'T STAND ON YOUR OWN TWO FEET.
DON'T MAKE A DIFFERENCE.
DON'T MAKE FRIENDS THAT LAST A LIFETIME.
DON'T FIND OUT WHAT YOU'RE CAPABLE OF.
DON'T BECOME A BETTER YOU.

Search Army Jobs

ARMY
BE THE BEST

RESEARCH QUESTION
Exploring meaning

This research task involves you collecting some written or spoken texts in order to further explore a particular section of this chapter you have found interesting. Here are some ideas to get you started:

- Explore the British National Corpus (freely available at www.cambridge.org/links/esctex6011) to investigate particular usages and collocations of words and phrases. Try out some words that you think are 'neutral' and see if your predictions are true or false.

- Use www.cambridge.org/links/esctex6012 to collect a range of political leaflets. What kinds of metaphors do the text producers draw on, and why might this be? What kinds of source/target domains are used – and are there any emerging patterns? You could compare the use of metaphor across two political parties, or investigate one political party in close detail. Or, choose a particular event or topic (e.g. a referendum, healthcare, or education) and explore the types of metaphor used.

- Collect a series of adverts for products or services. What kind of future or alternative world do they project? For example, do they project the text receiver as a benefactor of the product or service? How are these projections actualised through language? Do they use modality or negation, for example? What kind of background and schematic knowledge does the text assume of its audience?

Wider reading

The following books and chapters all provide good introductions to semantics and the study of meaning:

Depraetere, I. and Reed, S. (2006) 'Mood and modality in English'. In B. Aarts and A. McMahon (eds) *The Handbook of English Linguistics*. Oxford: Blackwell.

Griffiths, P. (2016) *An Introduction to English Semantics and Pragmatics*. Edinburgh: Edinburgh University Press.

Lakoff, G. and Johnson, M. (1980) *Metaphors We Live By*. Chicago: University of Chicago Press.

Semino, E. (2008) *Metaphor in Discourse*. Cambridge: Cambridge University Press.

Chapter 5
Spoken language

In this chapter you will:

- Examine the patterns, organisation and functions of spoken language

- Explore some ways in which politeness and impoliteness are exhibited in language

- Analyse various features of spoken interaction, and how speakers construct meaning

5.1 Working with spoken language

Up to this point we have largely focused on written texts, and so we now turn our attention to spoken language. For most people, speech is the dominant mode of communication, and we spend far more of our time speaking and listening than we do reading and writing. Speech is clearly different from writing in a number of ways: it is typically spontaneous, it is the chosen channel of communication when people are face-to-face, and it cannot be edited or deleted. Whereas writing is a human invention that requires a tool (such as a pen or a keyboard), speech is largely thought to have developed naturally.

5.2 Speech acts

Language gets things done, and is highly performative – things that we say can have enormous bearings on things in the world, changing people's futures, statuses and perceptions in a number of ways. Consider how these short utterances change the world:

I now pronounce you husband and wife.

You are hereby sentenced to life imprisonment.

We would like to offer you the job.

Each of these is an example of a speech act, where there is a specific intention behind the utterance, that impacts upon the world. In the first example, the speech act changes the legal status of two people and performs a specific event that brings about tangible change. Of course, the speech act must be uttered by the right person at the right time – I am not a qualified registrar, and could not change the legal marriage status of two people by simply telling them they are now husband and wife. These conditions and contextual requirements are known as felicity conditions.

KEY TERMS

Speech act: an utterance considered as an action that does something

Felicity conditions: the conditions that a performative speech act must meet if it is to be appropriate or successful

According to John Austin (1975), there are three elements of felicity conditions.

- Firstly, there should be a conventional procedure for what is being carried out.

- Secondly, the participants within the event need to fulfil their roles properly – in our marriage example, we would need a professionally qualified registrar and two willing people that wanted to marry each other.

- Thirdly, all participants must have the necessary thoughts and intentions, in what are known as sincerity conditions: people must be sincere about what they are saying. For example, if a speaker says 'I'm really sorry I haven't finished the homework' when they have failed to complete a piece of set homework, and they are *sincerely* sorry that they have failed to do so, then the sincerity conditions have been met. If they are not genuinely sorry, then this is not a legitimate apology. Of course, we cannot always know whether speakers are fulfilling sincerity conditions: we cannot accurately read people's minds and people can be good at pretending!

> ### KEY TERM
>
> **Sincerity conditions:** a type of felicity condition that requires speakers to be sincere about what they are saying

There are various ways of classifying speech acts as a whole, but perhaps the most useful is by John Searle (1969) who proposed five groups:

- **Assertives**: these commit the speaker to believing something, e.g. *believe, suggest, put forward, swear, boast, conclude.*

- **Directives**: these try to get the hearer to perform an action, e.g. *ask, order, request, invite.*

- **Commissives**: these commit the speaker to doing something in the future, e.g. *promise, plan, vow.*

- **Expressives**: these express how a speaker feels about something, e.g. *thank, apologise, welcome.*

- **Declarations**: these change the state of the world in certain ways, e.g. *I resign, you are fired, I plead guilty.*

Finally, all speech acts can be direct or indirect. A direct speech act is where the meaning of the utterance is literal – for example, a person asking her friend 'Do you want to go to the pub tonight?' is a genuine question seeking a genuine response. Picture the same two friends – one of them says 'Could you pass me the water?'. Despite its interrogative form, its function is a directive: the speaker is not really asking whether she is physically able to 'pass the water'. This is an indirect speech act, where the meaning of the utterance depends upon context and the hearer's ability to understand the implicature behind the utterance. Two further examples are:

It's quite cold in here (indirectly uses a directive, e.g. *turn the heating on*)

That was silly of me (indirectly uses an expressive, e.g. *I apologise*)

We often use indirect speech acts, in attempts to be polite and not to impose too much on those around us. Section 5.5 explores this in more detail.

KEY TERM

Implicature: the implied or intended meaning of a speech act

5.3 Narrative

A narrative is essentially a story, a re-telling of events that are either real or imaginary. We will look at oral narratives here, and use William Labov's 1972 model of narrative structure as a framework. The appeal of this model is that it arose out of normal, everyday discourse of real speakers in real situations. Labov analysed a corpus of hundreds of narratives and found a recurring structural pattern, which he organised into six categories. Each of these categories fulfils a different role or function in the narrative, and they are listed in Table 5.1. I have invented a very short narrative to illustrate each category.

The categories occur in the sequence that they would normally do in natural narrative, apart from 'evaluation' which can appear at any point. It may be useful to think of evaluation functioning as a kind of adverbial, in that it has a flexible position and provides additional information about other parts of the narrative. It tends to sit 'outside' the main narrative and is important in explaining the relevance of the story itself. In the evaluation category in Table 5.1, the speaker provides an opinion on the event, providing a reason and motivation for wanting to tell the story.

Not all narratives will include all six categories, and the order of them may slightly change, but Labov's model is a useful and fairly robust one nonetheless. You could try applying the model to narratives you hear or read, and test it out against things that weren't included in Labov's original corpus: newspaper articles and literary fiction, for example.

Table 5.1: Labov's narrative categories (adapted from Simpson, 2014: 115)

Narrative category	Narrative question	Narrative function	Linguistic form	Example
Abstract	What was this about?	Signals that the story is about to begin and catches the attention of the listener	A short statement, provided before the narrative begins	So
Orientation	Who or what are involved, and when or where did it take place?	Helps the listener to identify the time, place, people, activity and situation of the story	Typically uses past continuous verbs and adverbs of time, place and manner	me and mum were out looking for Christmas presents
Complicating action	What happened next?	The core narrative category providing the main bulk of the story	Temporally ordered clauses with a verb in the simple past or present	and we bumped into a friend from school who I haven't seen in years
Resolution	What finally happened?	Recaps the final key event of the story	Expressed as the last of the narrative clauses that began the Complicating action	turns out she lives just around the corner about two streets away
Evaluation	So what?	Makes the point of the story clear; expresses an opinion about the story	Intensifiers, modal verbs, negation, repetition, embedded speech, comparisons with unrealised events	I couldn't believe it, what are the chances of that
Coda	How does it all end?	Signals that a story has ended	A generalised statement which is 'timeless' in feel	funny how things turn out isn't it

5.4 Multi-speaker interaction

Next, we consider spoken language that involves more than one participant, which we can call conversations, or multi-speaker interaction. This involves participants collaborating and jointly negotiating meaning, taking turns and interrupting each other along the way. Just like written language, spoken language exhibits patterns and conventions that can be analysed in detail.

5.4.1 Turn-taking

Generally, people collaborate successfully during a conversation and achieve what they set out to do. Speakers take turns to offer their own thoughts at the right time and allow other people to speak, in what is known as the turn-taking system. The simplest pattern of turn-taking is an adjacency pair, consisting of two turns by two different speakers, in response to one another. This will often be a question-answer structure:

A: shall we get a takeaway tonight?

B: yes please!

> **KEY TERMS**
>
> **Turn-taking:** the process by which speakers co-construct conversation
>
> **Adjacency pair:** a simple structure of two turns

In this example A and B cooperate together in conversation, and B's response is expected, in what is called a preferred response. If B had responded with something unexpected or irrelevant, then this would be a dispreferred response. However, human conversation is not always as straightforward as simple turns like these, and turns are often added before the sequence is completed:

A: shall we get a takeaway tonight?

B: good idea! what are you thinking?

A: maybe Indian?

B: yes please!

Here, B's first turn is a request for more information, to which A responds. This is called an insertion sequence. Often, the beginning and ending of a turn is indicated by a discourse marker, which are words like *well, like, of course, yeah,*

Text Analysis and Representation

right, and *oh*. As well as marking the beginning and end of turns, discourse markers carry several other functions:

- For a speaker to show the listener that they are listening

- Creating solidarity with the listener

- Appealing to the listener for understanding and showing how the speaker feels.

KEY TERMS

Preferred response: a second part of an adjacency pair that fits in with what the speaker of the first part wants to hear

Dispreferred response: a second part of an adjacency pair that doesn't fit in with what the speaker of the first part wants to hear

Insertion sequence: an additional sequence between the two parts of an adjacency pair

---

Generally, we get along well, and people are skilled at anticipating the boundaries of turns so that they begin speaking as soon as (or before) their interlocutor has finished. Of course, people often interrupt or overlap one another – if they are keen to convey how much in agreement they are, or keen to challenge or add something of their own. This is known as holding the conversational floor, where speakers negotiate who is speaking when, and give cues that they want a response from their interlocutor. Cues can be given by interrogatives, use of direct names, dropping intonation, pauses or body language such as open-handed gestures. Try and notice these things when next having a conversation with somebody. How do speakers hold the floor? How are the boundaries between turns established? Do interruptions and overlaps suggest agreement or disagreement? To illustrate, look at Text 5A, where two friends discuss the merits of living in Barcelona compared to England:

Text 5A

Rob: it's not that cold (.) but it does get cold cos the (.) it gets very wet and windy

Cat: yeah mhm I used to

Rob: but you can only compare it with the summer over here you can't compare it with

Cat: yeah but

Rob: cos when you're over there it seems colder than it would normally do

Cat: yeah

Rob: cos it's icy and so windy (.) really windy there by the sea

Cat: right

In this short exchange, it is clear that Rob holds the floor and dominates the conversation. He speaks more than Cat, even though they have the same number of turns. Cat repeatedly tries to take a turn by overlapping ('yeah mhm I used to'; 'yeah but') but this is largely ignored by Rob, who perseveres. Cat employs a number of backchannels (see Table 5.2) to show that she is listening, but seems more interested in seeking a way to get her turn in rather than asking Rob further questions or details.

> **KEY TERM**
>
> **Conversational floor:** the 'space' containing a conversation. Participants can share this floor, or hold the floor in attempts to control a conversation

5.4.2 Non-fluency features

Although we might have an idea of what we want to say, most conversations are unplanned and naturally occurring speech is peppered with hesitations, repetitions and sounds that you would not find in the dictionary. Together these are known as non-fluency features and have a range of functions – from giving speakers a chance to think, for dramatic effect, to highlight what is coming next, and so on. Pauses are a common non-fluency feature, and can be made up of silence or fillers such as *hmm*, *erm*, or *like*. In Text 5B, pauses under a second are represented by a dot in a bracket, for example (.) and pauses over a second are represented by the number of seconds in a bracket, for example (2).

Text Analysis and Representation

KEY TERMS

Non-fluency: features of speech that disrupt or repeat spoken discourse

Filler: a non-verbal sound that acts like a pause

Text 5B

> erm so I mostly listen (.) I listen to R&B (1) I must admit that I have some dodgy tracks (3) I've got a spice girls number on there (.) wannabe I think (.) erm (.) just because it reminds me of school (.) hmm (.) well got out of (.) which (.) what about you?

Here, the speaker pauses to think as he remembers details about his past, and hesitates to admit some of the 'dodgy tracks' he feels embarrassed about. Fillers such as 'erm' and 'hmm' also indicate his apparent uncertainty and unwillingness to talk about his taste in music. There is also an example of a repair, where he corrects himself and starts again, in what appears to be a move to shift the focus away from himself:

> 'well got out of (.) which (.) what about you?'

Repairs occur for a number of reasons: remember that speech is often spontaneous, and so speakers do not always get it 'right' on their first attempt. They might be a grammatical mistake, or the speaker may have chosen the wrong word to express what they mean.

Speakers might also use a false start, which is a little bit like crossing out in writing, as in:

> So I mostly listen (.) I listen to R&B

Here, the speaker begins to speak, stops and then starts again. The second attempt allows the speaker to clarify his intended message.

KEY TERMS

Repair: when a speaker corrects some aspect of what they have said

False start: when a speaker begins to speak, stops and then starts again

---

5.4.3 Other features

There are lots more features of spoken language, some of which are listed in Table 5.2:

Table 5.2: Features of spoken language

Feature	Definition and function	Example
Tag question	A question structure that usually consists of an auxiliary verb + pronoun, and is usually placed at the end of a declarative. It typically conveys a negative or positive attitude towards something, or can be used to seek verification.	She's late, *isn't she*? It's at 9 p.m., *is it*?
Hedge	Words that imply a sense of vagueness, evasiveness, are non-committal, express imprecision or down-tone the meaning of the following word.	I'm *sort of* annoyed with him It's *more or less* the same price We *might* come home at the weekend
Backchannel	Sounds, words, phrases or body language that show feedback, in terms of attention or agreement. May be used to encourage a speaker to carry on talking, or to imply boredom or frustration.	*I guess so* *mhm* <nods head>
Deixis	Words that refer to an object or person in the immediate context that is shared by participants (the deictic centre).	I will have *this* one please. Can *you* bring *that* over *here*?

Text Analysis and Representation

Feature	Definition and function	Example
Conversational historical present	Use of the present tense in an account of past events, to emphasise a sense of vividness or immediacy.	I was in town yesterday and *this bus crashes straight into a car*
General extender	Words and phrases such as *and stuff, and things* and *something* that indicate the previous word is part of a set, or to be purposefully vague, or when a speaker assumes that the participants know what is being referred to.	We went swimming *and stuff* I'd like some clothes *and things*
Intensifier	Adverbs such as *very, really* or *well* which add emphasis to the word it precedes.	That is *well* cheap It's *right* cold The bus was *really* fast
Phatic communication	A function of language to maintain or develop social relations between speakers. Phatic communication is perhaps most noticeable during the beginnings or endings of conversations, and sometimes thought of as 'small talk'.	*Hello, how are you?* *Have a nice day* *Nice weather today, isn't it?*

ACTIVITY 5.1

Transcribing and analysing speech

Record a few minutes of natural conversation between two people, making sure to ask permission first. Then, transcribe the speech as accurately as possible, following the conventions to mark non-fluency (pauses, fillers, interruptions, etc.). Analyse the finished transcription for its spoken language features: narrative categories, adjacency pairs, the features in Table 5.2, and so on. Make sure to not just label parts but try and explain why things are there and what their presence indicates. Think carefully about the relationship between the participants and the context in which the conversation takes place, and how this affects language use.

5.5 The social nature of speech

Speech is a social activity, and for the majority of the time it allows us to communicate with other people with relative ease and efficiency. It can be tiring, and frustrating – especially when language is misinterpreted or we struggle to convey or understand an intended message. In this section, we look at how speakers show politeness and impoliteness, and how they use language collaboratively.

5.5.1 Politeness and impoliteness

Why do we bother being polite? Why do we bother with phatic communication, which has no real semantic meaning and only serves a social function? Why do we worry about how we make requests, ask questions, or the way we address somebody? Why do we rely on implied meanings rather than literal ones? An interesting and useful way of exploring such questions is through the concept of face, meaning 'self-respect' or 'dignity' and most commonly associated with the work of Erving Goffman (1969). The theory suggests that due to our highly social lives, we depend upon one another to get things done and are concerned about how we appear to other people. In trying to get things done, we try to do so without losing face and we try to look after other people's face at the same time. Essentially, face theory is about ways of being polite and impolite.

5.5.1.1 Face

For sociolinguists, the most interesting development of face theory is by Penelope Brown and Stephen Levinson (1987), who distinguished between positive face and negative face. Positive face is the desire to be liked and appreciated, concerned with solidarity and respect between speakers, when language shows approval for other people's behaviour. Negative face is the desire not to be imposed or intruded upon, when language exhibits respect for other people's rights and maintains a distance from them. Both positive and negative face can be threatened, in what are called face-threatening acts (FTAs). If something threatens our positive face, then we feel embarrassed or ashamed. If our negative face is threatened, then we feel offended. There are five kinds of FTA:

1 Do an FTA directly, with no politeness (e.g. 'Do the washing up, you lazy thing!').

2 Do an FTA with positive politeness, by attending to the hearer's positive face needs (e.g. 'You are so good at helping around the house. I just wish you were better at washing up.').

3   Do an FTA with negative politeness, by attending to the hearer's negative face needs (e.g. 'I know you're very tired and overworked but I would appreciate it if you could do the washing up.').

4   Do an FTA indirectly, or off-record (e.g. 'I wonder how long it's been since you did any washing up?').

5   Don't do the FTA.

KEY TERMS

Positive face: a universal human need to feel valued and appreciated

Negative face: a universal human need to feel independent and not be imposed upon

Face-threatening act: a speech act that has the potential to damage someone's self-esteem either in terms of positive or negative face

Speakers can choose how much they attend to each other's face needs depending on context: their own social relationship, the degree of power between them, or the degree of imposition. Whereas most research on spoken language has focused on how speakers try to maintain levels of politeness, the linguist Jonathan Culpeper has tried to provide an 'impoliteness framework', which is in parallel to Brown and Levinson's work. Culpeper (2011) identified a series of strategies that are orientated towards attacking face. Underlying these is the importance of context, and that certain things are only impolite depending on the situation of use. A fundamental aspect of context when discussing im/politeness is the social and power relationships between participants. Some of the strategies are:

- Mock impoliteness, or 'banter': impoliteness that remains on the surface, since it is understood by others not to cause offence.

- Ignoring or snubbing your interlocutor, by excluding them from a conversation or refusing to engage with them. This could be through silence, or by the use of obscure or secretive language that is designed to mystify others.

- Appearing uninterested, unconcerned or unsympathetic.

- Actively seeking disagreement by selecting a sensitive topic.

- Making your interlocutor feel uncomfortable, for example by not avoiding silence or not using small talk.

- Using taboo words: swearing, abusive or disrespectful language.

- Using personal negative evaluations, e.g. *you can't do anything right*.

- Invading personal space, either literally by positioning yourself closer than the relationship permits, or metaphorically, by asking for information which is too intimate given the relationship.

- Dismissals: explicitly telling your interlocutor to leave or stop talking.

- Being sarcastic.

ACTIVITY 5.2

Language in the boardroom

Text 5C is an extract from *The Apprentice*, a reality TV show in which contestants compete for a job with Alan Sugar, a successful UK businessman. At this point, the contestants are in the boardroom and discussing the failure of a task. Analyse the transcript by using models of im/politeness and face theory as a framework. It may be easier to do this for each participant individually, and then summarise your findings.

Text 5C

A = Alan Sugar

B = Ben

P = Paula

A: what was the point you were making as a human resources manager then?

P: because you got (.) a person here who works in finance and a person who runs a restaurant

A: but **you** were the team leader (.) **you're** the team leader

P: I understand that (.) but my skills are in creativity and…

A: mm (2) it's a feeble excuse as far as I'm concerned (.) you put yourself up to come in this process and you're now using the excuse that you're a human resources manager so therefore **you shouldn't be in charge of costings** (.) If that's the case why did you put yourself in charge of costings?

P: I **didn't** put myself in charge of costings Sir Alan (.) which is why I nominated two people to look after my costings

B: I think the bottom line here (.) is that if you'd wanted me involved with those costings (.) then it's a failure on your part as the project manager for not saying Ben can you come round here and look at it and just make sure it's alright

P: surely an idiot would have worked that out

B: **we're talking about idiots now?** well let's talk about 5 pounds and 700 pounds if you wanna talk about costings at the end of the day you made **a complete balls up of it** you were the ones responsible for the cock up in the fragrances you were the project manager you were the one who should have come to me getting involved in the costings if you wanted to and

P: I asked you to

B: and the next day I **sold my bloody heart out** for you just to do damage control

P: the cost of the fragrances was a cost it wasn't a cost on its own I asked you to look after costs and you didn't

A: ok who should I fire then?

B: **Paula** should be fired

5.5.1.2 Conversational maxims

Underlying the notion of im/politeness, intention, performance, speech acts and felicity conditions is the 'cooperative principle', which is the assumption that speakers intend to mean things and hearers accept this in trying to work out what is being said. Paul Grice (1975) suggested that when engaging in conversation, people follow four 'rules' or maxims, complying with general principles and protocols for managing and negotiating discourse events.

- **Maxim of quantity**

  Make your contribution to the conversation as informative as necessary.

  Do not make your contribution to the conversation more informative than necessary.

- **Maxim of quality**

  Do not say what you believe is false.

  Do not say that for which you lack adequate evidence.

- **Maxim of relevance**

  Say only things that are relevant.

- **Maxim of manner**

  Avoid obscurity of expression.

  Avoid ambiguity.

  Be brief (avoid unnecessary wordiness).

  Be orderly.

Grice did not mean for his maxims to be rules for speakers to learn, but a set of tools for analysing dialogue. In order to decode the communicative intention of others, people draw inferences about other people's state of mind – based on the linguistic forms used and an assumption that people generally adhere to the four maxims. In conversation then, speakers generally observe the maxims, and listeners generally assume that speakers are observing them. When the maxims are broken, they can create implicatures, which are implied meanings that have to be inferred by a text receiver as a result of the maxim being broken or

ACTIVITY 5.3

Exploring maxims

Work out which maxims are being violated in the following examples (there may be more than one in each example). Some context is given to help you do this. For each one, try and explain why you think the speaker(s) have chosen to violate the maxim.

1   Conversation between a parent (P) and teenage child (C):

    P: where are you going?

    C: out

    P: what time will you be home?

    C: later

2   Conversation between two strangers waiting for a delayed train:

    A: you can always trust the rail system in this country

    B: it's such a reliable service isn't it

3   Conversation between a customer (C) and a hotel receptionist (R):

    C: is there a problem with the internet in my room?

    R: not that I'm aware of

C: the connection seems a little funny

R: perhaps it's your computer?

C: no, it was working fine before I arrived

4   The beginning of a telephone conversation:

A: hi is that Mr Clarke?

B: no

5   Conversation between a parent (P) and a young child (C), who has just spilled paint over the floor:

P: what's happened in here?

C: I don't know

P: haven't you just been in here?

C: no I've been upstairs

P: so the paint pot just fell over by itself?

Next, rewrite each example so that no maxim is being violated. Give explanations for your changes.

violated. In a way, they are similar to indirect speech acts, which we looked at in section 5.2.

When conversational maxims are violated, the speaker is deliberately drawing the hearer's attention to a form of implicit meaning. When conversational maxims are abided by, participants are engaging in prototypical conversation.

Of course, a person's understanding of the maxims and what constitutes them being violated depends on culture. Grice was American, and theory was based on his observations of Western conversations. Within this culture, there are obviously still differences, as in Text 5D. This is part of a conversation I had with a waitress in New York City, on my first visit to the USA, whilst trying to order some breakfast.

Text 5D

Me:	I'll have the fried eggs and toast please
Waitress:	ok how do you like your eggs
Me:	erm (.) just fried is fine thanks
Waitress:	yes is that sunny side up

Me:	(1) what does that mean
Waitress:	it means the yolk sits on the top
Me:	oh ok (.) yes that's fine
Waitress:	and the toast (.) we have white, rye, sunflower seed, pumpernickel

And so the conversation went on, for a number of minutes. For me, a native British speaker with little experience of visiting the USA, saying 'fried eggs and toast' was a simple and direct speech act that I assumed would get the job done. In American culture however, it is not so simple. For the waitress, my order was a violation of the maxims of manner and quantity: I had simply not given enough information to fulfill the requirements, and so my utterance was ambiguous and vague. For me, it felt like the same maxims were being violated for different reasons – I had no understanding of the complex ordering system in the USA, there was nothing on the menu to indicate that there was such a choice of fried eggs and toast available, and I am not used to ordering such specific ways of food being prepared. Indeed, in Britain I am often apologetic when asking for variations in my order, keen to attend to employees' negative face needs in worrying that my request will be too much of an imposition, whilst in the USA it is the norm. The poor waitress who had to deal with my limited cultural knowledge of USA food ordering practices became frustrated with this and my indecisions about what type of eggs and bread I wanted.

5.5.2 Contexts and cultures

How do we handle the vast array of social situations and contexts we find ourselves in, and how does this shape the language that we choose to use? Peter Stockwell (2002) suggests the notion of scripts for our linguistic behaviour in different social contexts. Scripts are sets of 'guidelines' or social codes for how we use language according to the situation we find ourselves in. Stockwell gives an example of a 'pub script', based on his experiences of visiting different types of pubs in the UK. A script is activated upon entering a specific social context: so, when walking into a British pub, we know that there will be familiar objects and people (beer, tables, a person behind the bar) and expected ways of behaving with language. This includes ordering drinks at the bar (as opposed to waiting at a table, as is the European convention), and knowing what kind of conversation topics are likely and deemed 'appropriate' for such a situation. In Text 5D, part of my failure to order breakfast was a result of my lack of script knowledge of American restaurants. However, scripts are not static: as I spent more time in the USA, my script knowledge was updated and expanded so that by the time I left, I knew exactly what to say and what questions I was likely to be asked.

In summary, the study of politeness and impoliteness is essential to the study of social interactions. It connects aspects of linguistic identity, social contexts and linguistic forms, and can be thought of as linguistic behaviours that are positively or negatively evaluated in a particular context. These behaviours can be positively evaluated because they attend to someone's face needs, or negatively evaluated because they attack somebody's face. The degree of your understanding of culture influences linguistic behaviour and has an outcome on what is construed as im/polite.

5.5.3 Using language to think together

When speakers engage in conversation, it is often not just for sharing information and interacting socially, but to work together to solve problems. When they do so, they engage in what Neil Mercer (2000) calls *interthinking*. Mercer claims that language is not just a tool for sharing knowledge, but a tool for 'thinking together'. Interthinking is defined as the 'joint, coordinated intellectual activity which people regularly accomplish using language' (2000: 16). It views language as more than just the mere transmission of thoughts from one person to another, seeing communication as a collaborative meeting of minds, or a 'mental-matrix' (2000: 105). The concept of interthinking is influenced by the psychologist Lev Vygotsky (1962), who distinguished betwen *intermental* activity (social interaction) and *intramental* activity (individual thinking). So, students in a classroom discussing a poem, for example, engage in dynamic intramental and intermental thinking to collaboratively construct meaning. Mercer proposes three types of interthinking: *cumulative*, *disputational* and *exploratory*:

- Cumulative interthinking is where people are in agreement with one another – talk that is uncritical, uncompetitive and constructive. They will largely attend to others' face needs.

- Disputational interthinking is where participants are in disagreement with each other. Talk may be characterised by arguments, insults and other face-threatening acts.

- Exploratory interthinking is talk where participants are interested in reasoning and evaluating, and jointly making sense of the world. In this type of talk, discussions are constructive yet critical and typically make use of *because*, *if* and *why*, where speakers are accounting for their opinions and engaging in co-reasoning with each other.

Text 5E is a conversation that took place between two builders, who are discussing a job:

Text 5E

Philip:	they've got three things, a sink, a bath and a corner shower on the other side, right
Rob:	in that one room
Philip:	yes it's wider than this room
Rob:	no way (.) absolutely not
Philip:	it's (.) it's wider than this room, and it's easily from here to the end of the kitchen
Rob:	no it's not (1) whata load of rubbish Philip, no, that's an exaggeration, come on, it's about as wide, it's as long as this room
Philip:	I'm telling you mate (.) you don't have a clue
Rob:	mate you are mad (.) how can you possibly think that

Text 5F is a transcript from a Year 7 (age 11–12) English lesson, where the teacher (T) and class are discussing reading. Zara (Z) and Nawar (N) are students.

Text 5F

T:	alright then year seven let's hear what you have to say then (.) so first question was how is reading like seeing (.) who's got any ideas about what we mean by that Zara

Zara: I think it's true because when you read you see lots of things because of the describing words in the book and you can kind of imagine the scene

T: ok so when you read something that's very descriptive you can imagine what's there

Zara: yeah if it's a good book I mean

T: do people agree with Zara

Nawar: I think it's sort of seeing but more like imagining

T: ooh interesting reading is imagining

Nawar: yeah because I imagine what something would look like

Text 5G is a conversation between two friends, in their 30s, who are out shopping in a market.

Text 5G

Lily: I wonder when they're gonna do the renovations for the market, did you see that in the papers?

Sam: yeah it's brilliant isn't it

Lily: they're gonna have lovely trees, it's gonna be very quaint (1) have you finished all our fruit?

Sam: ooh yes

Lily: do you want some grapefruit?

Sam: good idea yeah let's get a couple

Lily: okay two grapefruits as well then, erm, bananas are still thirty, do you want to get a couple of bananas? It's so cheap isn't it (1) I love shopping at markets like this

Sam: it's lovely (.) so much nicer than going to the supermarket

RESEARCH QUESTION
Exploring spoken interaction in detail

On the internet, find an example of unscripted multi-participant interaction and choose a two-minute sequence from this. Some useful contexts might be:

- A debate between politicians in the House of Commons

- A TV documentary interview between presenter and guest(s)

- A tabloid talk show (e.g. Jeremy Kyle)

- A dating show

Transcribe your chosen clip using the appropriate conventions and then explore the following:

- Describe the context and the relationship between participants.

- What features of spoken language are used, and why might this be the case?

- Can you analyse the transcript in terms of face theory?

- Do the speakers observe Grice's maxims? Do they flout these at any point? Why? How might you account for this in terms of power relationships between participants?

- Analyse how language is used to negotiate and co-construct meaning. What types of interthinking can you observe, and why might these be present?

- What about body language? What does this signal about each speaker?

Wider reading

Read more about spoken discourse by exploring the following books:

Cameron, D. (2001) *Working with Spoken Discourse*. London: SAGE.

Jones, R. (2016) *Spoken Discourse*. London: Bloomsbury.

Stenström, A. (2014) *An Introduction to Spoken Language*. London: Routledge.

Ideas and answers

Chapter 1

Activity 1.1

There is no clear 'answer' for this: the key lies in justifying your choices, providing textual evidence to do so. For example, Text 1A would be towards the formal end of the cline due to its impersonal nature, marked through the lack of personal pronouns such as 'I' and 'you', which removes any sense of human authorship from the text.

Activity 1.2

The text-world that the language triggers will be different to everyone, but is likely to be built from particularly salient patterns of nouns ('beach', 'waterfront', 'jet skis', 'castle', etc.), adverbs and prepositional phrases, which place things in particular points in space ('either side', 'up and down', 'within', etc.). The text-world will also be fleshed out by readers' own background knowledge and memories of such places.

Activity 1.3

Again, this will be different for everybody. The 'rules' may be explicit (e.g. codes of conduct for how to dress at work) or implicit (e.g. social codes and rules relating to power and authority). Creating groups of words and phrases that are particular to each discourse community is particularly illuminating when discussing register and how language changes across different contextual spaces.

Activity 1.4

The text exploits a number of stereotypes about the male discourse community: primarily that they do not like talking about their feelings. The world-view of males projected in this text is firstly that men have their own 'secret' language, suggested through 'propamanda' and 'mandictionary', in what is an instance of intertextuality: where a particular genre 'borrows' or refers to typical conventions of another genre (in this case, the dictionary genre). The text goes on to play on the wider discourse of the social stereotypes of men: being 'manly' and 'laddish', and how perhaps males are expected to fulfil these characteristics in their behaviour in order to be a 'valid' member of the male community. Text 1G overtly reinforces these social stereotypes and discourses, and the two texts together provide an interesting comparison in the representation of men.

Activity 1.5

This rewriting activity could be done in a number of ways, but more successful ones are likely to be ones where the commentary provides evidence of conscious decision making and clear justifications for shaping language in particular ways. A good starting point would be to research the genre you are trying to recreate the text into, by reading some texts from this genre and discussing the language choices, patterns and conventions.

Chapter 2
Activity 2.1

Remember that phonetic transcription is based on sound, not spelling – students should try and ignore the way that words are spelled and focus on pronunciation instead. The transcriptions should look like this:

television	/teli:vɪʒən/
knife	/naɪf/
password	/pɑːswɜːd/
charge	/tʃɑːdʒ/
thumb	/θʌm/

Note that 'password' and 'thumb' have been transcribed using Received Pronunciation – /pæswɜːd/ and /θʊm/ would be perfectly acceptable variations.

Activity 2.2

This extract makes extensive use of sound iconicity:

- use of consonance in 'curt cuts', where the plosive sounds /k/ and /t/ mimic the accuracy, precision and sharpness of the spade

- consonant clusters and onomatopoeia in 'gravelly ground', 'squelch' and 'slap' represent the noise that the metal spade makes when it digs into the earth, as it hits stone, mud and water. It could be argued that the complexity and intricacies of the speech sounds mirrors the randomness of the rural earth. Note the high number of consonant clusters in the phonetic transcription: /grævəliː graʊnd skweltʃ slæp/. The vocal articulators move in complex and difficult ways, in the same way that the spade does as it tackles the earth.

Activity 2.3

The text uses the second person singular 'you' to point directly to the reader, in what is an example of synthetic personalisation (Fairclough, 2001) – where the reader is made to feel as if they are being addressed personally – even though there is no social relationship between text producer and text receiver. The end of the text uses the first person plural 'we', suggesting that text producer and text receiver share similar values and world-views.

Practice question

Particularly interesting things to look out for include:

- Mumbai represented as a chaotic, busy city of extremes and contrasts.

- Use of varied nouns and noun phrases to populate the vivid world of Mumbai: 'dreamers', 'starlets', 'gangsters', 'stray dogs'.

- Use of superlative adjectives to indicate the extreme qualities of Mumbai: '<u>biggest</u> slums'; '<u>most expensive</u> home'; '<u>largest</u> tropical forest'.

- Patterns of relational verbs, which gives a repeating listing quality about Mumbai: 'Mumbai is big'; 'Mumbai is India's financial powerhouse'; 'It has India's most prolific film industry'.

Chapter 3
Activity 3.1

Many of the noun phrases include reference to human relationships ('two people'; 'diversity of connections'; 'two opposing forces'; 'dual-faceted scent'), suggesting this fragrance has the potential to bring people together. References to locations and landscapes are also plentiful: 'urban woody fresh fragrance'; 'magnetic woods'; even though 'urban' and 'woods' are clearly very different places, the perfume claims to be representative of both. Note also the references to energy: 'thrill of life'; 'opposing forces'; 'electric freshness'.

Activity 3.2

Note how it is always a human/humanity referent that appears in subject position: 'no one'; 'this world'; 'men'; 'they'. Of course, these humans are being watched by the (as of yet unspecified) Martians – but we do not know who or what they are yet. This means that humans remain the focus of attention – much in the same way that the Martians are focusing their attention on them from outer space. The Martians remain unspecified ('intelligences') and are passivised: for example, in the clause 'this world was being watched' and 'they were scrutinised and studied'.

Chapter 4
Activity 4.1

Words that activate schemas will vary from reader to reader, but are likely to be nouns related to money ('wealth'; 'power'; 'money') and health ('flat-belly powerfoods'; 'energy'; 'nutrition'; 'fitness'). These schemas are likely to contain information and world knowledge about lifestyle choices and a specific consumer group – males; business and city workers in the financial sector; people concerned with looks and self-image. Audiences that have a limited schematic knowledge of these things are unlikely to be consumers of the magazine.

Activity 4.2

Some of the metaphors used to represent political parties, the country and its population are:

A COUNTRY IS A PERSON	*Britain was on the brink; Britain is back on its feet; Britain […] growing stronger every day*
UP IS GOOD	*Britain is back on its feet*
BRIGHT IS GOOD	*clear economic plan; brighter […] future*
SMALL IS GOOD	*halved our deficit*
ECONOMY IS A SUBSTANCE	*fastest growing major economies in the world; clear economic plan*
EMPLOYMENT IS A CONTAINER	*more people are in work*
FORWARD IS PROGRESS	*we have turned things around; put our country back on the right track*

Activity 4.3

The ideal consumer of the text is someone who is patriotic, sympathetic to the army, and looking for a career change. Here we have a series of negated imperatives, which set up a series of conceptual spaces or 'worlds' in which the text receiver imagines what it would be like to join the army, and therefore not be a 'better you'. The final two imperatives ('search army jobs'; 'be the best') snap the reader out of the negated spaces and set up the final world, set in the future, where the text receiver has done exactly what the imperatives commanded of them (searched 'army jobs') and is now 'the best version' of themselves. The imperative world 'works' because the text receiver has had to go through all of the negated worlds in order to get there. They have seen what life could be like if they don't join the army – and decided to go ahead and join. The final state is the reader comparing two different versions of themselves: one having not joined the army; one having joined it.

Chapter 5
Activity 5.1

This activity is designed so that you can see some of the difficulties and complexities involved in speech transcription. The likelihood is that there will be a wide range of spoken language features – working through each one systematically is the best way to handle the amount of data your transcription will have created. When analysing the data, make sure to try and relate your interpretations to context. When and where was the conversation recorded? What is the relationship between participants? How might your presence as a researcher have affected the data?

Activity 5.2

- As the powerful participant in this heated situation, Alan threatens other people's positive face on a number of occasions, most notably through the use of personal negative evaluations ('it's a feeble excuse as far as I'm concerned') and direct questions ('why did you put yourself in charge of costings?').

- When Paula's positive face is threatened by Alan, she attempts to deal with this by first trying to deflect attention from her inability to do the costings, instead promoting her own creative skills ('my skills are in creativity'). When Ben threatens her face directly ('it's a failure on your part as the project manager'), she responds by using personal negative evaluations ('surely an idiot would have worked that out').

- Ben responds by using a range of impoliteness strategies that threaten Paula's face: actively seeking a sensitive topic ('if you wanna talk about costings'); taboo language ('you made a complete balls up of it') and dismissals ('Paula should be fired').

Activity 5.3

1 C violates the maxim of quantity, in not specifying the details of where they are going and what time they will be home – information that (presumably) is desired by P.

2 Given the context, both speakers use sarcasm to violate the maxim of quality, in that they express things that they believe to be false.

3 C is clearly seeking some assistance and for the hotel to address the problem, rather than being told they/their computer is to blame. Thus, they violate the maxim of manner, and also the maxim of relevance.

4 B violates the maxim of quantity (we would expect B's answer to explain who indeed *is* speaking) and manner (because it remains ambiguous who B actually is).

5 In this context, we (and probably P too) know that C is guilty. C is clearly trying to avoid being reprimanded for something they know they have done wrong, and attempts to achieve this by violating the maxim of quality (the utterances are lies).

Practice question

- Text 5E takes place in an occupational context and involves a disagreement between two people, who we assume are co-workers. The interesting thing about this text is the way that the participants use deictic markers to try and describe the space they are no longer in, often comparing it against their current context: 'wider than this room'; 'shower on the other side'. The participants use personal negative evaluations (e.g. 'mate you are mad') but these are attached to politeness markers such as 'mate' to try and maintain a close social distance.

- Text 5F is in an educational setting, where the teacher is the marked powerful participant. The teacher uses direct names and singular/plural pronouns to try and involve the class, and select who contributes to the discourse. Student responses are given praise (e.g. 'ooh interesting') to try and encourage them further.

- Text 5G is a social context between two participants who clearly have a narrow social distance between them. This is indicated by: the fluent adjacency pairs (question > answer) which have preferred responses and the relatively 'equal' conversational floor. Lily asks three questions which suggests she leads the discourse, whereas Sam responds positively to each suggestion and question, asking only one question (in the form of a tag: 'it's brilliant isn't it') which could be argued as a sign of her seeking verification for her contributions.

Transcription key

(.)	indicates a pause of less than a second
(2)	indicates a longer pause (number of seconds indicated)
Bold	indicates stressed syllables or words
: :	indicates elongation of a word
((*italics*))	indicates contextual or additional information
[ ]	indicates the start and end points of simultaneous speech

References

Austin, J. L. (1975) *How to Do Things with Words*. Oxford: Clarendon Press.

Baker, P. (2006) *Using Corpora in Discourse*. London: Continuum

Baker, P. (2014) *Using Corpora to Analyze Gender*. London: Bloomsbury.

Bates, E. (1979) *The Emergence of Symbols*. New York: Academic.

Brown, P. and Levinson, S. (1987) *Politeness: Some Universals in Language Usage*. Cambridge: Cambridge University Press.

Cameron, D. (1995) *Verbal Hygiene*. London: Routledge.

Crystal, D. (2006) *Language and the Internet*. Cambridge: Cambridge University Press.

Culpeper, J. (2011) *Impoliteness: Using Language to Cause Offence*. Cambridge: Cambridge University Press.

Depraetere, I. and Reed, S. (2006) 'Mood and modality in English'. In B. Aarts and A. McMahon (eds) *The Handbook of English Linguistics*. Oxford: Blackwell, pp. 269–290.

Fairclough, N. (2000) *New Labour, New Language?* London: Routledge.

Fairclough, N. (2001) *Language and Power*. London: Routledge.

Fairclough, N. (2003) *Analysing Discourse: Textual Analysis for Social Research*. London: Routledge.

Gee, J.P. (2014) *An Introduction to Discourse Analysis: Theory and Method*. London: Routledge.

Giovanelli, M. (2014) *Teaching Grammar, Structure and Meaning*. London: Routledge.

Goffman, E. (1969) *The Presentation of Self in Everyday Life*. Harmondsworth: Penguin.

Grice, H. P. (1975) 'Logic and conversation'. In P. Cole and J. Morgan (eds) *Studies in Syntax and Semantics III: Speech Acts*, New York: Academic Press, pp. 183–98.

Hall, S. (1973) *Encoding and Decoding in the Television Discourse*. Birmingham: Centre for Contemporary Cultural Studies, University of Birmingham.

Hodge, R. & Kress, G. (1994) *Language as Ideology*. London: Routledge.

Kövecses, Z. (2002) *Metaphor: A Practical Introduction*. Oxford: Oxford University Press.

Labov, W. (1972) *Sociolinguistic Patterns*. Oxford: Blackwell.

Lakoff, G. (1987) *Women, Fire, and Dangerous Things*. University of Chicago Press.

Lakoff, G. and Johnson, M. (1980) *Metaphors We Live By*. University of Chicago Press.

Mercer, N. (2000) *Words and Minds: How We Use Language to Think Together.* London: Routledge.

Ogden, C.K and Richards, I.A. (1923) *The Meaning of Meaning*. Orlanda: Harcourt Brace. Jovanovich.

Pope, R. (1995) *Textual Intervention: Critical and Creative Strategies for Literary Studies*. London: Routledge.

Rosch, E. (1975) 'Cognitive representations of semantic categories', *Journal of Experimental Psychology: General* 104: 192–233.

Rosenblatt, L. (2005) Making *Meaning With Texts: Selected Essays*. London: Heinemann.

Searle, J. (1969) *Speech Acts*. Cambridge: Cambridge University Press.

Simpson, P. (2014) *Stylistics: A Resource Book for Students* (Second edition). London: Routledge. Routledge.

Stockwell, P. (2002) *Cognitive Poetics*. London: Routledge.

Vygotsky, L.S. (1962) *Thought and Language*. Cambridge, MA: MIT Press.

Glossary

accent: variation in pronunciation associated with a particular geographical region

active voice: where the subject is filled by an agent, who performs the action expressed by the verb

actual writer: the real person or people responsible for text production

adjacency pair: a simple structure of two turns

adjective: a word that modifies a noun phrase

adjective phrase: a phrase that has an adjective as its head word

adverb phrase: a phrase that has an adverb as its head word

adverb: a word that modifies a verb, an adjective or another adverb

adverbial: an optional part of the predicate, whose function is to identify the circumstance of the verb phrase in terms of place, time or manner. It is usually an adverb or a prepositional phrase

anaphor: a linguistic unit that is defined by its antecedent

antecedent: a linguistic unit from which another unit derives its interpretation

audience positioning: how different audiences are targeted by text producers, which results in different interpretations of a text

auxiliary verb: a verb belonging to a small class which accompanies other verbs

blended-mode: a text which contains conventional elements of both speech and writing

boulomaic modality: expressions that highlight aspects of desire

bound morpheme: a morpheme that cannot stand on its own

cline: a continuum used in linguistics to indicate a range of a particular language feature: formality, literariness, mode, etc.

collocates: words that typically appear together

complement: the attribute of a subject or object

compounding: the formation of a new word from two or more existing words

conjunction: a word that connects similar or different units together

connotation: the overtones associated with a word or phrase

consonance: a pattern of repeated consonant sounds for effect

construal: the ability that language has to represent/perceive the same thing in different ways

context: the background against which a text conveys its meaning

contextual parameters: specific time, location, person and function details about the context of a text: *when*, *where*, *who* and *why*

conversational floor: the 'space' containing a conversation. Participants can share this floor, or hold the floor in attempts to control a conversation

coordinator: a word that links words, phrases and clauses together where they are equal

declarative: a sentence that has a typical function to make a statement

deixis: words that are context-bound and whose meaning depends on who is using them, and where and when they are being used

denotation: the literal or primary meaning of a word

deontic modality: expressions that highlight a sense of obligation or necessity

derivation: the way that a morpheme helps form a new word

descriptivism: a view of language that is concerned with describing language in use

determiner: a word that appears before a noun phrase and helps to give it some definition

diphthong: a vowel sound that is the combination of two separate sounds, where a speaker moves from one to another

discourse: the analysis of a) how language in use creates meanings; b) natural language occurring in different social contexts; c) how language is used as a form of social practice

discourse community: a group of people involved in and communicating about a particular topic or issue, that typically share values, world-views and ways of using language

discourse event: an act of communication occurring in a specific time and location involving writers/speakers and readers/listeners

dispreferred response: a second part of an adjacency pair that doesn't fit in with what the speaker of the first part wants to hear

ellipsis: where one or more words are omitted

epistemic modality: expressions that highlight degrees of belief, certainty or perception

exclamative: a sentence that has a typical function to make an expressive or emotive exclamation

face-threatening act: a speech act that has the potential to damage someone's self-esteem either in terms of positive or negative face

false start: when a speaker begins to speak, stops and then starts again

felicity conditions: the conditions that a performative speech act must meet if it is to be appropriate or successful

filler: a non-verbal sound that acts like a pause

foregrounding: drawing attention to a key aspect in a text

form: labels given to describe what linguistic units *are* (word classes, phrases and clauses)

free morpheme: a morpheme that can stand on its own and can usually form a word in its own right

function: labels given to describe what linguistic units *do* (subject, object, adverbial, etc.)

genre: a way of grouping texts together based on expected shared conventions

head word: the most important, pivotal word in a phrase

imperative: a sentence that has a typical function to issue a command

implicature: the implied or intended meaning of a speech act

implied writer: the authorial presence projected by a specific narrative

infix: a morpheme that appears inside a root word to modify its meaning

inflection: the way that a morpheme shows a grammatical category such as a verb tense or a plural noun

insertion sequence: an additional sequence between the two parts of an adjacency pair

interjection: a word whose function is purely emotive

interrogative: a sentence that has a typical function to ask a question

intertextuality: a process by which texts borrow from or refer to conventions of other texts for a specific purpose and effect

intransitive verb: a verb that does not take an object

lexical verb: the main, most meaningful verb in a sentence

main clause: a clause which bears no relation (other than through coordination) to another clause

metalanguage: language about language

metaphor: a structure that presents one thing in terms of another

modal verb: an auxiliary verb that joins with a main verb to show the degree of commitment towards an event or person that a speaker holds

modality: a system of meaning related to a speaker's attitude to, confidence in, perception about something in the world

mode: a meaning-making system or channel of human communication

morpheme: a unit that makes up a word

morphology: the internal structure of words

multi-clause structure: a structure constructed from more than one clause

negation: an act of denial, a negative statement, a refusal or contradiction, marked through linguistic forms such as *no*, *not* and *never*

negative face: a universal human need to feel independent and not be imposed upon

non-fluency: features of speech that disrupt or repeat spoken discourse

noun: a word that names a physical thing or abstract concept

noun phrase: a phrase that has a noun as its head word

object: often the entity being acted on by the action of a verb process, so they refer to a different person or thing than the subject. They can be nouns, noun phrases or pronouns, and normally come after the verb phrase. There are two kinds: direct and indirect.

onomatopoeia: words that have some associated meaning between their sound and what they represent

participants: the text producer(s) and text receiver(s) involved in a given discourse event

passive voice: where the subject is filled by a patient, who receives the action expressed by the verb; the agent is omitted or placed later in the clause

phoneme: an individual speech sound

phonetic alphabet: a system for showing the inventory of different speech sounds in a language

phonetics: the area of study that is concerned with investigating how sounds are produced by language users

phonology: the area of study that refers to the more abstract sound system

phrase: a group of words that is grammatically connected and defined by its head word

polysemy: where words, phrases or texts have many possible meanings, often as a result of the text producer/receiver's cultural background and world-view

positive face: a universal human need to feel valued and appreciated

powerful participant: the participant that holds the most power in a given discourse and context

pragmatics: the branch of linguistics concerned with language in use– including how context shapes meaning, choices and interpretations

predicate: what is left of the sentence when the subject has been removed, representing what the subject is about (compare with *rheme*)

preferred response: a second part of an adjacency pair that fits in with what the speaker of the first part wants to hear

prefix: a morpheme that appears before a root word to modify its meaning

preposition: a word that shows connections between other words, often showing a sense of place or time

prepositional phrase: a phrase that has a preposition as its head word

prescriptivism: a view of language that is concerned with standards and correctness

pronoun: a word that substitutes for a noun phrase

pronoun system: the way that pronouns (either of the same or different sub-classes) work together to create meaning in a text

rank scale: a way of showing how smaller units of language are built up to create larger ones

register: a variety of language that is associated with a particular situation of use

repair: when a speaker corrects some aspect of what they have said

representation: the portrayal of events, people and circumstances through language and other meaning-making resources (e.g. images and sound) to create a way of seeing the world

rheme: a part of a sentence communicating information related to whatever is indicated by the theme

schema: a bundle of knowledge about a concept, person or events

script: a conceptual structure used to understand linguistic and behavioural protocols in various situations

semantic field: groups of words that relate to a set of meanings for a particular topic

semantics: the branch of linguistics concerned with the study of meaning. This includes the meaning of words and their combinations into larger structures (phrases, clauses and sentences)

sincerity conditions: a type of felicity condition that requires speakers to be sincere about what they are saying

social proximity: the perceived remoteness between participants and groups – for example, a married couple have a very narrow social distance, whereas a shop keeper and a customer have a wide social distance

sound iconicity: the matching of sound to an aspect of meaning

speech act: an utterance considered as an action that does something

split discourse: where communicating participants are separated in time and/or space (for example, an email exchange, a postcard, a phone call, a text message, a book, an advert)

subject: often the instigator of a process expressed in the verb phrase. It is usually a noun phrase, noun or pronoun (compare with *theme*)

subordinator: a word that links clauses together to show one is dependent on another

suffix: a morpheme that appears after a root word to modify its meaning

syntax: the study of how words form larger structures such as phrases, clauses and sentences

text producer: the person or people responsible (through writing and speaking) for creating a text

text receiver: the person or people interpreting (through reading or listening to) a text

text-world: a conceptual representation (or mental image) of language that is created by linguistic content and individual knowledge

theme: a part of a sentence corresponding to what the sentence as a whole is about

transitive verb: a verb that takes one or more objects

turn-taking: the process by which speakers co-construct conversation

verb: a word denoting actions, states or events

vocal articulator: a different part of the vocal tract involved in the production of speech sounds (e.g. lips, tongue, alveolar ridge, vocal folds)

voicing: the vibration of the vocal folds in the production of speech. Voiced sounds are those made with vibration; unvoiced sounds are those without vibration.

word class: a category (or type) of word that behaves in the same way in a sentence

Index

Acknowledgements

The authors and publishers acknowledge the following sources of copyright material and are grateful for the permissions granted. While every effort has been made, it has not always been possible to identify the sources of all the material used, or to trace all copyright holders. If any omissions are brought to our notice, we will be happy to include the appropriate acknowledgements on reprinting.

Text 1E Extract from Virgin Trains FAQs used by permission of Virgin Trains; Text 1G Front cover image from Men's Health Magazine used by permission of Wright's Media; Text 1H Advert used with permission from Campaign Against Living Miserably; Text 2A Excerpts from 'Digging' by Seamus Heaney, from New and Selected Poems 1988–2013 by Seamus Heaney Reprinted by permission of Faber and Faber Ltd., and from OPENED GROUND: SELECTED POEMS 1966–1996 by Seamus Heaney. Copyright © 1998 by Seamus Heaney. Reprinted by permission of Farrar, Straus and Giroux; Text 2E Reproduced with permission from the Lonely Planet website www.lonelyplanet.com © 2017, Lonely Planet; Text 3D Voucher used by permission of City of London Police; Text 4C from the Conservative party manifesto and website; Text 4F Crown copyright information taken from the British Army advertisement. Used with permission under the terms of the Open Government Licence (OGL); Text 5C extract of transcript from The Apprentice, aired by the BBC, produced by Boundless, part of Freemantle Media

Development of this publication has made use of the Cambridge English Corpus (CEC). The CEC is a multi-billion word computer database of contemporary spoken and written English. It includes British English, American English and other varieties of English. It also includes the Cambridge Learner Corpus, developed in collaboration with Cambridge English Language Assessment. Cambridge University Press has built up the CEC to provide evidence about language use that helps to produce better language teaching materials.

Thanks to the following for permission to reproduce images:

Cover image Emanuel Rossi / EyeEm/Getty Images; chapter opener images 1–5 Hero Images/Getty Images, Grant Faint/Getty Images, xxmmxx/Getty Images, Busà Photography/Getty images, Craig Taberner/Getty Images; all other photographs © Ian Cushing

The publisher would like to thank the following members of The Cambridge Panel: English who assisted in reviewing this book: Annette Brady, Sagarika Bhatia and Pramod Kanakath.